Praise for *Every Word Matters*

'In *Every Word Matters*, Ranjana Srivastava takes up the most important question for any writer who wants to make change in the world: who are you writing for? With the rich and compelling stories that have made her *Guardian* column a joy to read for years, this little book is a masterclass, filled with the essential writing tips, tools and strategies for finding and using your voice as a writer.'

**Alex Green, Harvard Kennedy School,
author of *A Perfect Turmoil***

'In a smart and insightful how-to manual that upends a traditionally dry genre, Ranjana Srivastava gives us a window into the process, puzzles, risks and rewards of writing essays, op-eds and advocacy pieces. Drawing on her own rich career as a physician-writer, she takes readers behind the scenes to elucidate key motives, steps and missteps and helps them plan for the potential reactions when their writing takes on a life of its own. A skilled and compelling storyteller, Srivastava carries readers along, demonstrating essential writing strategies even as she articulates them, offering many spoonfuls of delightful sugar to help the instructional medicine go down.'

**Debra Malina, Perspective Editor,
*New England Journal of Medicine***

'Dr Srivastava's columns have always made me think philosophically about what it means to live a meaningful life, although she is never didactic. This is writing with a clear and strong heartbeat, that places the human being at the centre of the story.'
Alice Pung, author of *Unpolished Gem*

'A piece of writing from Ranjana Srivastava is a gift. Few full-time writers, let alone physician writers, ever achieve the clarity, truthfulness and courage that have become the hallmarks of Srivastava's work. I always learn something from reading her words; she helps me see my patients and my work anew.'
Melanie Cheng, author of *The Burrow*

'Ranjana Srivastava is a natural storyteller with a faithful following among readers. Her empathy and kindness, as well as her fierce intelligence and deep knowledge of her profession and the human condition, shine through in everything she writes. Any aspiring writer would benefit from the clear-eyed and compassionate advice in this book.'
Svetlana Stankovic, Opinion Editor, *Guardian* Australia

'Many doctors write. Few write as well as Dr Ranjana Srivastava. I have always thought that there is something therapeutic in her essays. Reading this book, I realise that her writing is part of her vocation, a vocation that can be taught as one can teach a student to read an EKG or chest X-ray. In *Every Word Matters*, Srivastava articulates the power, and value, of writing.'

**Adam Cifu, MD, University of Chicago,
co-editor of Sensible Medicine**

'In *Every Word Matters* Ranjana Srivastava warmly welcomes readers into her journey from aspiring writer to columnist, offering an honest account of the rewards and challenges of her work. Srivastava's candid exploration of the writing process is surprisingly relatable. She provides guidance on how writers can make space to write, seek the human angle in complex topics, weave evidence into compelling narratives, and cultivate a vibrant practice fuelled by curiosity and consistent reading. Packed with helpful tips and example columns, this book is an inspiring read for both budding and seasoned columnists.'

**Lauren Brodsky, Senior Director,
Communications Program,
Harvard Kennedy School,
co-author of *Because Data Can't Speak for Itself***

Every Word Matters

Every Word Matters

Dr Ranjana Srivastava

SIMON & SCHUSTER

New York · Amsterdam/Antwerp · London · Toronto · Sydney · New Delhi

EVERY WORD MATTERS: WRITING TO ENGAGE THE PUBLIC
First published in Australia in 2025 by
Simon & Schuster (Australia) Pty Limited
Level 4, 32 York St, Sydney NSW 2000

10 9 8 7 6 5 4 3 2 1

New York Amsterdam/Antwerp London Toronto Sydney New Delhi
Visit our website at www.simonandschuster.com.au

© Ranjana Srivastava 2025

All rights reserved. No part of this publication may be reproduced, stored in a retrieval system, or transmitted in any form or by any means, electronic, mechanical, photocopying, recording or otherwise, without prior permission of the publisher.

A catalogue record for this book is available from the National Library of Australia

ISBN: 9781761634192

Cover design: Luke Causby/Blue Cork
Typeset by Midland Typesetters, Australia
Printed and bound in Australia by Griffin Press

The columns and essays by the author have been reproduced with kind permission of the *Guardian*, the *Lancet* and the *New England Journal of Medicine*.

The paper this book is printed on is certified against the Forest Stewardship Council® Standards. Griffin Press holds chain of custody certification SCS-COC-001185. FSC® promotes environmentally responsible, socially beneficial and economically viable management of the world's forests.

For Swati
Childhood friend;
lifelong inspiration

Contents

Introduction: The Necessity of Brevity		1
1:	Routine and Discipline in Writing	11
2:	Finding a Topic	25
3:	Who Am I Writing For?	40
4:	How to Build a Column	52
5:	Crafting a Strong Start	63
6:	From Thinking Clearly to Writing Clearly	73
7:	Simplifying Complex Topics	88
8:	Developing your Writing Career	102
9:	Writing for the Public	118
10:	Storytelling and Consent	132
11:	What to Know About Sharing Personal Details	146
12:	Tackling Sensitive Issues	159
13:	Protest Writing	169
14:	When Writing Offends	180
15:	How to Navigate Criticism	191
16:	Seeking and Using Feedback	204
17:	Why You Need an Editor	218
18:	The Work and the Joy of Writing	231
Acknowledgements		241
About the Author		243

Introduction

The Necessity of Brevity

> 'A writer is someone for whom writing is more
> difficult than it is for other people.'
> Thomas Mann

When I was a medical student in Australia in the early 1990s, my parents lived in a small city in the east of India, where my father was a university professor of physics. My parents found themselves on an excruciatingly slow government waiting list for a landline phone connection, with no certainty of ever receiving one in their university-issued house.

I was a homesick teenager. To bridge the distance, I would write to them on aerogrammes, which were prepaid and limited to a single page. It also meant limiting a lot of information to that page. My short letter took more than a month to reach my parents, rendering the news outdated by the time it arrived. So, it felt like I was always preparing the next batch of writing, not knowing that this would become a lifetime habit.

On their side, my parents faced an even greater challenge. Where they lived, aerogrammes weren't easily available and the post office was far away. A significant breakthrough came when their immediate neighbour reached the top of the queue for a phone connection. Now, I could call the neighbour, who would summon my parents from across the fence. My parents would scurry to the neighbour's home, but our conversations lasted just minutes, more a way to fulfil the longing to hear each other's voice than truly connect. If I had a specific reason for the call – to give them the date of my flight home or to ask for a recipe – I had to speak clearly and listen closely. And still, those fleeting phone calls could cost more than a week's groceries.

Fast forward 30 years, and I've lost count of how often I talk to my parents. Not to mention the constant exchange of text messages, banter in group chats, and the sharing of adorable dog photos. The transformation from those days of scarcity to our present abundance feels like a godsend. But those dim experiences of communicating with my parents with limited resources would enforce a habit of clarity and brevity that I now value as a writer.

As I embarked on a career in medicine, the ability to distil complex information into its essence became a necessary skill. When treating a sick, and often fearful, patient, it is essential to cut through the jargon and convey the core message concisely and sensitively. But first, this requires an understanding of the issues, deciding in one's own mind what is fact, opinion, misconception and myth, and then finding the right words and right style of communication.

On to writing. How I wish I had thought of a delightful observation often attributed to Anton Chekhov a hundred years before I was born:

> Medicine is my lawful wife, and literature is my mistress. When I get fed up with one, I spend the night with the other. Though it is irregular, it is less boring this way, and besides, neither of them loses anything through my infidelity.

The Necessity of Brevity

I have always regarded writing as my personal passion, a creative endeavour I have pursued for the sheer joy of tinkering with words. Writing is my happy place.

My true calling, my vocation, is medicine. I am an oncologist. No one would imagine my job as being 'fun', but it is deeply satisfying and thought-provoking to get to help patients at one of the darkest times in their lives.

Being an oncologist also involves a form of exposure – from the time you walk out to the waiting room, people watch the way you treat the clerical staff, greet patients, whether you help carry their belongings or offer to push their wheelchair, how you respond to a flock of anxious relatives.

Inside a clinic room, each turn of phrase, every nuance, indeed every facial expression is scrutinised by worried and hopeful patients and their loved ones. It is a privilege and a sacred responsibility to be in a position of providing hope, solace and care to people facing a challenge that is equal parts medical and existential.

People enter medicine to make a difference. Typically, doctors do so through clinical practice, research, teaching and volunteering and I, too, have done each of these. But as my career advanced, I realised what I enjoyed most was a chance to democratise medicine through writing. To take the complexities of an illness or the convolutedness of the healthcare system and articulate it to the average person struggling to make sense of things, or simply curious to learn more, seemed like a worthwhile goal, one that I enjoyed, stuck to, and never resented, even when the long working hours bled into each other.

There is some routine and drudgery in all work but when I write, that feeling disappears. It is a place where I can be in a state of flow. I also keep growing, learning and meeting people I would never otherwise have.

Since 2013, I have had the joy of being a columnist for the *Guardian* newspaper, where I write on the intersection of medicine and society, or more broadly speaking, the art of medicine. Founded in 1821, the *Guardian* is one of the world's oldest English language newspapers and has attracted many noted contributors. I like to say that I fell into this job through sheer persuasion but that would be to undersell my effort, and unfair to you, the reader. So, I will expand on this in the pages to come.

My favourite quote about the *Guardian* comes from a former editor, CP Scott: 'Comment is free but facts are sacred.' This thinking resonates with me as a doctor, and I have tried to adhere to it as a writer.

The *Guardian* opened my eyes to a whole new dimension of writing opinion and advocacy pieces. Suddenly, I had a public platform. Committed to my 'real' job and still inclined to think of myself as an accidental journalist, I vividly recall meeting Katharine Viner, the *Guardian*'s editor-in-chief, in London in 2018 and seeing, for the first time, a printout of the metrics of my columns. How many people read my column, how many minutes they spent on it and which country they were reading from. The metrics demonstrated the impact of my writing in granular, sometimes uncomfortable detail. Sometimes my voice was amplified by international exposure and other times, arguments horrifyingly took on a life of their own.

But most of all, I was struck by the technology that allowed me inside these metrics. The editor-in-chief said approvingly that people read my column till the end. *Why wouldn't they?* I thought innocently. As a medical student I was conditioned to read entire textbooks without regard to my interest. It's how one passed year upon year of exams. As an avid reader, I am in the shrinking category of the mistakenly loyal who plod through boring books until the end. So, it really was a revelation to me that anyone would *not* spend the seven or eight minutes to read my column in full.

I now cringe at my naïveté, but perhaps the mistaken assumption of an early, devoted audience helped me become a more committed writer. When the truth dawned on me, it proved a welcome liberation to write how I wanted without blanching at the thought of being read (and judged) by a lot of people.

I had been writing for some years by then, but my London meeting was the first time it sank in that I wasn't just writing for myself. My columns frequently featured in the 'most popular' section of the day, a few were the 'most read' of the year across the entire *Guardian* platform, and in 2023, one of my columns became the top trending column around the world on Apple News. I discovered this when my brother texted me while travelling in India ('Is this you?', despite the name and photo) and my children saw notifications on their phone in Australia.

A regular column written every two weeks might attract between 25,000 to 50,000 views; but when a topic touches a nerve, the readership can jump into the millions. Whatever the number, over a lifetime of writing, it would surpass the potential number of patients I could treat in my entire career, even if I were to work well into old age. *This* is the power of writing for the public.

But penning occasional pieces of good writing isn't enough for people who want to influence the public discourse. I am still experimenting with ways of getting better and I will share my experiences with you throughout this book.

As a doctor, I am surrounded by facts. Anyone familiar with an academic journal knows that you can't read past a paragraph without bumping into a citation. Academic writing is typically dense, sterile and process oriented. It swims in evidence, citations and references. I rely on academic writing to treat my patients, but while helping to progress a field, this kind of writing often strips away the human element.

Writing opinion and advocacy pieces for the public is different. To write compellingly (and keep people reading to the end) requires adding back the human element.

The first question I ask myself about every column is, 'What's in it for the reader?' Because if I can't make it matter, the reader will click past.

For someone who is curious about a lot of subjects that I would like to write about, the notion of putting the reader first doesn't always come naturally, but by now, I have worked with enough reputable editors and publishers to learn its primacy.

The Covid pandemic served as a powerful reminder of the importance of effective communication. The challenges and emotional turmoil experienced by patients and professionals cannot be underestimated and I was proud to serve on the frontline of healthcare, confronting its stark realities. Those difficult years shone a light on the importance of compassion and empathy, but also vitally important and, indeed, lifesaving, was clear communication from all the stakeholders.

Before the pandemic, finding interesting healthcare topics to write about had never been a challenge. However, the pandemic brought a fresh influx of pressing issues that deserved attention. Driven by purpose, I felt my voice grow stronger.

Each column felt like an extension of service to society, aiming to bridge the gaps in knowledge, foster understanding, and challenge preconceived notions. I saw how effective communication by my colleagues and me played a crucial role in explaining important ideas, pre-empting questions and facilitating understanding. Invitations to talks on communicating with the public helped me hone my skills and learn from other people.

In 2022, shortly after completing a degree in public administration at Harvard, I was invited to teach writing at the Harvard Kennedy School and Harvard Medical School. Always up for a challenge, I accepted and saw the great interest many professionals have in writing for the public.

I so enjoyed teaching and grading papers to help other people write better that I developed an elective writing course for medical students at the University of Chicago and one for ethics fellows there, who were enrolled in the same ethics fellowship that I had completed in 2004. The people who asked me to teach these courses understood the increasing importance of teaching professionals how to write in a way to reach the public.

Today, I teach professionals who work in diverse fields including academia, government, education, medicine, the environment and engineering. They care about their subject, are passionate about making an impact, and have good ideas worth sharing. My job is to help them order their thoughts, give structure to their writing, and not let their initial enthusiasm for communicating with the public fade.

Like my students at Harvard and Chicago, people from all

over the world aspire to write but many lack the means to attend expensive courses or benefit from individual coaching and editorial assistance. For others, it is time, work and family commitments that make it impossible. Hence the idea of writing this book.

Its purpose is to share with you, the reader, what I teach in my classes: how to communicate with the public and advocate for issues you care about through clear, concise and compelling writing in fewer than 1,000 words.

In his foreword to Joan Didion's gem of a book of twelve short essays, *Let Me Tell You What I Mean*, the Pulitzer Prize-winning *New Yorker* critic and Columbia writing professor, Hilton Als, captures my own challenge of being a writer. He says that in reading a writer, you get two of them – the person who is saying something and the person who makes the words fit.

A newspaper or magazine column is typically 900 words. For a professional, this can seem like a woefully small limit to cover a lot of expertise. But this is the joy of writing – to pen a brisk column that touches the right notes, makes an impression, and may even be the starting point to changing minds. Most importantly, you want to write things you are proud of.

I am gratified when people dear to me enjoy my writing, but it is even more wonderful when complete strangers or my patients are touched by a column. To someone who feels very grateful for the opportunity to become a doctor when many other deserving individuals miss out, this really feels like a debt to society repaid.

Whether you are a fledgling writer or someone seeking to cultivate a regular writing habit, I want to draw upon my own experiences to help you write for the public. Together, we will delve into many topics, with each chapter written in approximately column length. In search of brevity, I have tried to take my own medicine.

In the pages that follow, you will find instruction, illustration and honest reflection. Where helpful, I have included my columns from the *Lancet*, the *Guardian* and the *New England Journal of Medicine*, the last two being the ones that publish me most frequently and have shaped me the most as a writer.

I have restricted myself to my own work not because I lack admiration for other writers. Indeed, it would be nice to include a variety of strategies and styles into a book like this, but it would be impossible to contextualise other people's writing and infuse them with the same immediacy as my own.

I know the impetus for every one of my columns, the process of composing and revising it, the range of responses, my own (sometimes visceral) reactions to those responses and the lessons drawn from the experience. I hope that this is what you will discover in the pages of my book, which therefore shows you *one* way of writing, not *the* way of writing.

I spent some of the most inspired years of my education in the United States, including my final year of high school in Pittsburgh, Pennsylvania. The man who taught English in the Pittsburgh Scholars Program at my school was a dry and exceptional teacher. By a stroke of luck, I was assigned to his 'lesser' class rather than the advanced placement class reserved for the best students.

Anyone who took Mr Sommerfeld's senior year English class will remember the unmissable poster at the front of the room that greeted us every day. On it was an empty, hard-backed chair. Beneath the chair these words: 'Alas, I would have been a better writer but the chairs in the library were too hard.' The poster teased, ridiculed and exhorted us to do better – and my classmates say that it did.

Reading this book will not turn you into a writer any more than padded chairs in the library will. But if you stay with me, are open to a bit of advice and guidance and, most important of all, ready to do the work of writing, I am confident you will emerge a better writer.

With that, I wish you good luck and happy writing.

1

Routine and Discipline in Writing

'If my doctor told me I had only six months to live,
I wouldn't brood. I'd type a little faster.'
Isaac Asimov

'How do you find the time?'

Everyone who is interested in writing has asked this question.

I am not unique in being armed with commitments: to my children and ageing parents, my medical work with increasing numbers of patients and stretched resources, friends and relatives whom I want to hold close, and my own needs. Still, writing is a ritual that I can't go without longer than a few days. Indeed, it is because I am busy that I write.

I think I was fond of writing even before I knew it. At age seven, growing up in India in an era of no television and months-long power outages, I was writing imagined dialogues between my dolls, of whom my parents had bought me a dozen, by candlelight. My dolls were my first audience: pleasant and willing accomplices to endless hours of storytelling.

I was ten years old when we moved from India to the English city of Liverpool, where I took an immediate liking to the lovely school principal, Mrs Atkinson, who warmly embraced me amidst the culture shock. Too dumbstruck to talk to her, or anyone else, I spent hours scribbling conversations I would like to have had with her and others. Liquid paper was in fashion, but I wrote so much that I constantly ran out of the little tubes, thus prompting me to write over my writing until the notebook filled up, at which point I would start all over again. My parents were puzzled by what kept me busy but probably secretly relieved I was occupying myself.

I didn't know anyone who wrote for pleasure, but I simply loved the feel of pen on paper. I have written a continuous diary since and entered my first poetry competition around that time.

After a year in Liverpool, we went back to India, where I returned to the familiar comfort of my old school and my old friends.

When I was fifteen, we moved again, this time to the United States. Here, I was lucky to be taught by a marvellous English teacher who ingrained in me the foundations of good writing. Mr Sommerfeld was an old-fashioned, no-nonsense teacher with a dry sense of humour, as evidenced by the poster I mentioned in the introduction.

He did not tolerate apathy but he also took genuine interest in the students who enjoyed his class.

'Put me there,' he would proclaim, asking us to transport him to the experiences, places and people we were writing about. It was his way of saying show, don't tell, and it was his phrase I took to heart and one that still echoes in my ears. I loved his class for its rigour and high expectations and it was the only 'writing course' I ever took.

He was thrilled to see me become a doctor and on my visits to the United States, I sought him out for lunch. I also acknowledged his powerful influence on my writing in my first book and in a *Guardian* column. Mr Sommerfeld died recently at age 90 and left behind a fine legacy, in that his students still remember him and save the papers he once graded.

Routine and Discipline in Writing

My break as a writer came as an Australian medical student in 1997 when, with my medical school professor's encouragement, I published a narrative in the prestigious journal, the *Lancet*, about an elective I had undertaken in my Indian hometown, which had burst my bubble of first-world medicine. I was left reeling, seeing my friends and other patients falling sick from preventable illnesses.

My publication was a hard-won prize because the editor had wanted to slash my essay by half, but my professor urged me to reply that his proposed edit would dilute my message. Quite happy to have my name associated with the *Lancet* in any form, I wrote to the editor just to appease my deeply invested professor and was surprised when he conceded that I had a fair point. My essay was published in full, and it was my very first lesson in standing up for the integrity of my writing.

Buoyed by that achievement, I began submitting to other publications, most of whom rejected my writing for not being strong enough, and once because the editor was also miffed at being mistaken for the editor of a rival publication. I was undeterred by the rejections, perhaps because I was finding solace in writing and quietly processing the big emotions I was encountering as a young doctor.

My friends expected that the demands of medicine would put paid to frivolities such as writing, but by then I knew what catharsis I could find in the act. I prioritised habit over content, grappling with questions that felt pretentious to ask aloud. *Who am I? Where am I headed? What matters?* People deal with the big questions of life in many ways. Some shop, run, drink, paint, see a therapist or talk to friends. From a young age, I weaved my way through life foremost by writing.

Writing for an audience

Writing for personal satisfaction takes discipline but ultimately, the stakes are low. No one will know or care if I am sparse with the truth, self-indulgent or boring. But every fortnight in the *Guardian* I submit 900 words for public consumption and judgement. Writing for the public entails care, complexity and responsibility. Therefore, this work, I think, calls for thoughtfulness, discipline and courage.

The heady part is having a public profile and harnessing the advantages of a public platform. In this way, my writing feels like an extension of service to society. The *Guardian* not being behind a paywall helps me gain global readership.

After reading my column, when an anxious patient is reassured, a harried relative feels heard, or a policymaker rethinks an issue, the feeling is indescribable. It brings a smile to my face when patients unexpectedly reveal that instead of telling their doctor how they felt, they printed out my column and left it for them to read and reflect on. And I still pinch myself when significant people in government, business or industry tell me that they enjoy my writing. But to borrow from Nietzsche that well-worn saying, even those who have a 'why' must find a 'how'.

The writing practice

Every writer, including those who 'love to write', requires discipline. There are no shortcuts. If you want to write effectively, you must create a deliberate practice. The students in my class recognise this and are eager to find a structure.

Here are some methods that have worked for me that you, too, might find useful.

Routine and Discipline in Writing

Firstly, writing needs dedicated time. Long ago, I decided that I couldn't treat patients every day because I need unstructured time to think and reflect. Filling every day with work and errands is a sure way to edge out the creativity and emotion needed to write. Obviously, this is a decision with career and financial implications, and not possible for everyone, but I believe that I am a better doctor (and a more balanced individual) for making time to write. This is one reason a physician friend of mine negotiated time to write and host a radio program when signing a university contract. I wish this were more common.

Another colleague finishes work and heads straight to a café for one hour before picking up her children from school and beginning her second shift of work. That one precious hour focuses her attention like a whole day might not. She once shared the mortified account of a fellow writer and mother who went to a seven day writing retreat, wrote seven words, and spent the rest of the time binge watching television. If I was ever given the dubious gift of unlimited writing time, I'd be in exactly the same boat.

I have since been glad to meet other professionals who have put a value on their writing and rearranged their work accordingly.

However, designating time away from work or other responsibilities is not enough, as it's far too easy to fill in time with other, undeniably important things such as seeing friends or getting enough sleep and exercise. After many years, the practice still doesn't just click into place; I must make time to write.

Just as writing requires designated time, the inspiration for a column doesn't just float up. For me, keeping a daily journal yields unexpected and valuable insights. Driving in silence helps me marshal my thoughts. And funnily enough, the rhythmic strokes of the rowing machine at the gym or a steady-paced run often help me 'write' a column in my head.

Since my column is published every two weeks, I am always writing. Each week, I try to allocate an uninterrupted block of four or five hours and incorporate additional deadlines. Behavioural economists call this 'choice architecture', to nudge the brain towards a desired behaviour.

I schedule a call or arrange to pick up a child close to a deadline, because a narrow window of opportunity to write forces me to focus. If I need to file a column during a holiday, I give myself a block of time when my teenagers are sleeping in; my reluctance to encroach on our time together makes my brain work harder and fingers type faster.

When it comes to minimising distractions, most people recognise their weaknesses. Mine is to stop worrying that in the very period my phone is on silent, my parents or children might need to reach me urgently. And I am not alone in fighting the urge to incessantly check my email and clear my inbox. In the course of my writing, many unnecessary emails have been written, junk folders examined and irrelevant surveys answered.

To make an idea tangible, I give my column a working title. Writing on two or three key points, I park the uncertainty of how they will fit together. Writing truly begets more writing. If you write down your first sentence, the second will come. Once you build the first paragraph, writing the next one is a little easier. The more you write, the more things fall into place.

I once innocently asked a prominent author if she ever experienced writer's block, thinking that it might be about the only thing we had in common. Memorably, she scoffed that no one asked a builder about 'builder's block' or expected a mid-flight pilot to suffer from 'pilot's block'. She said to regard any writing one wanted to accomplish as no different to a real job. Her no-nonsense attitude stayed with me. When I stop worrying about what to write or how my writing will be received and put my mind to doing the writing instead, I come out better.

Since I hate being reminded by my editor to cap my enthusiasm at 900 words, I adhere to a 1,000-word draft. I try to write as much as possible in one sitting and then set my work aside for a day or two.

On returning, I allocate another couple of hours for reading, revising and some mindless tinkering with words that nonetheless makes me happy.

I have grown more fluid with practice but it's very easy to waste time seeking endless perfection. To avoid this trap, I submit my column a few days before the deadline, which has the additional benefit of not being chased by editors and hence gaining goodwill.

A word about expectations: be forgiving. Sometimes, your designated time will evaporate. Or the words will feel wrong. Instead of being disheartened that the work of writing is beyond you, a commitment to trying again can be the inspiration to refocus and do better next time.

Apart from serving as a means of influence and communication, good writing is a gift to your readers. Keep moving.

TIPS

1. Pair interest with routine and discipline.
2. Clear away distractions.
3. Expect (and accept) small steps to success.

No Refuge for the Ailing

3 August 2006

New England Journal of Medicine

The still, oppressive heat of the afternoon seems to magnify the queue of waiting patients. A young woman separates herself from the crowd.

'Excuse me, Doctor, how long will you be?'

I answer with a flicker of annoyance, 'I am not sure, but I *will* see you.'

An hour later, it is her turn. She looks far too well, I silently judge. The well worried. She springs from her seat at the sound of her name but moves away from me toward the stairs. There, she utters a rapid command in a foreign tongue before turning apologetically toward me. Before I can greet her, a scarf-clad head comes into view. It belongs to an elderly woman physically supported by aides on each side. The aides stop on the landing, then wordlessly and cautiously lift her up to carry her into the only chair in my office. Her features are wizened, her frame more shrunken than the six decades indicated on her chart would predict. Her eyes are dull, opaque, her face a repository of apprehension, anxiety, perhaps worse. She periodically glances at her daughter, but mostly she keeps her face averted as we settle into the consultation. The daughter speaks for her.

'I am sorry if I was rude, Doctor. My mother has breast cancer, and she was waiting downstairs for a long time. We can't afford to see anyone. We need your help.'

I am caught unaware.

This is a refugee clinic, run out of a makeshift healthcare

facility as bare as any in the Third World. Volunteer physicians bring their own equipment and, often, spare drug samples. Limited numbers of doctors and meagre donations mean that we can barely treat hypertension, eczema and headache; we are rarely able to provide refugees with anything remotely resembling the standard of care.

We don't do cancer, I want to say, keen to end the conversation right there.

'Doctor, my mother has no one. We can't pay the specialists. The emergency room bills us if it doesn't turn us away. They said you would help.' Her tone combines pleading with frustration and accusation. The mother winces with pain. The daughter solicitously measures out some morphine. As the patient swallows it with a wry face, the daughter murmurs, 'This is the last morphine. We have to wait now until . . .'

'Until . . . ?'

'Until my husband's disability pension arrives.'

She brusquely runs her hand across the involuntary tears that have started. Her mother's hand surreptitiously reaches out to comfort her. In that moment, the enormity and heartache of the situation descend on me, and Mrs Habib becomes my patient.

Having lost all the male members of her family through war, Mrs Habib arrived from Afghanistan to live with her only daughter, an Australian resident. Here, her application for refugee status was denied on grounds of insufficient evidence, thus denying her access to any form of government support, including food, shelter, employment and healthcare. While the decision is appealed on humanitarian grounds, a process that can take years, the restrictions continue. Reliance on the family's small earnings worked until she developed cancer. A public hospital provided her with a free mastectomy but no follow-up. Now she is riddled with painful bony metastases. I read letters from physicians noting her inability to pay and theirs to continue her care. The documents mark a trail of disappointment.

I feel burdened by the realisation of what I am undertaking. How will I adequately stage or treat Mrs Habib's cancer? Where will her drugs come from? What will happen when she becomes terminally ill? The near-empty drug cupboard stares at me insolently. Reminders of past battles to achieve a modicum of care for less sick refugees fill me with a sense of foreboding. Distracting myself from the panic, I state aloud, 'First, we need to control your pain. Then we can think about other things.'

The clinic nurse locates an unused pack of donated morphine tablets and calls a local pharmacy to dispense morphine liquid at the clinic's expense. She also mentions a pharmacist who is willing to supply tamoxifen at cost. Mrs Habib still carries the prescription that she could never afford to fill. The nurse kindly reassures the daughter that the clinic will do everything it can to ensure Mrs Habib's comfort. I tell myself we will succeed.

'How long does she have, Doctor?'

'Without knowing the true extent of her disease, I can't really say.'

Fresh tears arise from the daughter's eyes. 'Can you see what it's like not knowing?'

I nod mutely, troubled by her grief and my growing concern.

A fortnight later, Mrs Habib is back, this time with severe headaches and vomiting.

'It must be the morphine,' I reassure her. 'She needs a full workup,' I chide myself.

The nurse sets about finding a laboratory that will run some basic tests free of cost – most claim that it is against their policy or simply refuse. Then, with patient and daughter watching, I receive a telephone call from the pharmacist who gave us the tamoxifen. He comes straight to the point.

'My colleagues warn that I could be de-registered for providing tamoxifen to an illegal. I have to get it back. And Doctor, perhaps you ought to consider how far you want to help these people – you are only starting out.' Appalled and incredulous, I fling the tamoxifen I was about to dispense into its box along with the near-expired bunch of donated inhalers.

'Thank God my mother doesn't understand English,' whispers the daughter, a mortified witness to the exchange. Anger, shame and remorse collide within me.

An hour of phone calls later, I have located a radiologist who agrees to sign off on a free CT scan of the patient's brain. He tells me he was once an immigrant himself. When Mrs Habib returns with a normal report, I am both relieved and disappointed. I have needlessly squandered a precious favour. The thought makes me feel petty.

Mrs Habib's vomiting persists. In the succeeding weeks, the clinic pays for a panoply of antiemetics, nutritional supplements and morphine, and her family resigns itself to her symptoms as a reality of cancer. But as the disease advances relentlessly in the absence of any treatment, another challenge arises, with an urgent need for palliative radiotherapy for her cancerous hip. The nurse worries that the clinic's money will run out if the heavy use of morphine continues. With a waiting list for radiotherapy at the best of times, I see little chance of convincing anyone to provide free service, but a few days later, we strike luck. As we bundle up a frail but grateful Mrs Habib, it seems inappropriate to remark on how fortunate she is.

The months pass, as she holds on precariously to life in the devoted care of her daughter. The refugee clinic becomes the family's sanctuary, a source of practical assistance and simple goodwill. Our supplies – of kind service providers and of donated funds – dwindle. By day, I bolster the daughter's hope that her mother will not suffer; by night, I fret with the nurse about how much longer we can sustain the promise we only half-manage to honour at the best of times. I watch the holiest of my aspirations, to comfort the sick, turn sour in the face of a woman who is a refugee first and a patient second.

On other days, my job as an oncologist seems far easier. I involve my other patients with breast cancer in treatment decisions that take advantage of an ever-expanding set of tools, and I am filled with a sense of gratification for both them and myself. I readily abandon medications in favour of others that may or may not be marginally better. 'It's worth a try' is the mantra of many desperate patients and their hopeful physicians. Multidisciplinary teams ponder their care, their suffering made all the more real by the noisy confluence of multiple opinions. To me, all the women look like Mrs Habibs. But the difference between Mrs Habib and other women with breast cancer is patently obvious. Those women are legal residents, their disease legitimate, and their care our duty.

But where, really, does our duty as physicians lie? Is it contained within the limits of what is convenient, or is every physician also an advocate? Is it conscionable to treat one patient with hundreds of thousands of dollars worth of drugs while another dies an inhuman death for lack of palliation? As borders worldwide become porous and more ordinary physicians in developed countries are exposed to sick refugees with neglected rights, the medical profession will increasingly be faced with the moral dilemma of addressing their health. As I cared for Mrs Habib, the vociferous political debate about refugees and their entitlements faded into the background, replaced only by the uncomfortable realisation that I was prevented from doing for one sick patient what I routinely did for others. I kept thinking what a hollow victory it seemed to laud the dizzying advancements in the profession while we turned a blind eye to the basic medical care of the disenfranchised.

Consumed by rampant disease and defeated by uncontrolled symptoms, Mrs Habib died one year after I met her. On the first anniversary of her death, I receive an unexpected call from her daughter, whose gratitude to the clinic remains undiluted. We speak fondly and emotionally of her mother, recollecting her brave fight. I wonder if the daughter has ever had the opportunity to discuss her mother's death. About to hang up, she says with utmost sincerity, 'Doctor, no one told me, but I know that my mother cost the clinic a thousand dollars each month. It must be good to have that money for other refugees.'

A stray reflex platitude freezes on my lips. The truth stings, but she is right.

About this column

This essay is akin to a firstborn. Writing in the *New England Journal of Medicine* is a holy grail for doctors, and I was overjoyed when my first-ever submission was accepted. I am embarrassed to think how many people I told this to who had no idea what the *Journal* even was.

This work was the fillip I needed to regard myself as *a writer* rather than someone who wrote. Refined and polished by a marvellous editor (more on this later), seeing it in print made me proud, happy and ambitious all at once. Once I had tasted the quality of a heartfelt piece rendered powerful by fine editing, I couldn't look back. As I will describe later, I have honed many of my skills through the *Journal*, which is why I maintain a personal goal of contributing one essay a year to a publication whose high standards and peer-review process keep me honest.

2

Finding a Topic

'The difficulty of writing is not in the writing itself,
but in the finding of a subject.'
Mark Twain

A writing professor once remarked that he knew many writers who talked a lot about writing and attended popular writing courses but had yet to produce any writing. This wry comment reminded me of the times I was eager to be a writer but not so sure that I could do justice to any writing. After all, every idea I had seemed to have been tackled by someone else with twice the aplomb.

When I listen to the professionals in my writing classes discuss some of their ideas, I feel eager to read their work, but first they must overcome a syndrome that I know all too well: 'Who, me?'

Self-doubt is real. Many people who excel in their field doubt their ability to convey their ideas or feel intimidated by the perceived ease of other writers. Writing for the public is to expose yourself to the public.

A good way to identify a subject to write about is to start with one's own interests and experiences. What topics am I drawn to? What unique perspective can I offer? What would I want to read?

In thinking about my own writing, I recently came across Norman Mailer's observation that writing requires a balance between confidence and humility. Too much ego and one risks being deaf to feedback; to have too little confidence is to be thwarted by self-doubt.

The best writing comes from a place of authority, authenticity and passion. There is a difference between cobbling together facts and powerfully describing an experience: both can fill a space, but writing on a topic you care about will make your heart sing and deliver the satisfaction, and even joy, of being memorable to the reader.

Expert writing that is straightforward and factual has a place. For instance, when reading a medical journal, I want the facts and stats outlined without 'window dressing' to help me help my patients. When I read the finance section of a newspaper about interest rates, and what they mean for my mortgage repayment, I hone in on the content.

But when writing to engage the public, your voice is just as, if not more important, than your knowledge: good writing illuminates a topic with your style and persona. It leaves people thinking – and wanting more.

I recently met a veteran GP with many insightful observations on the hapless state of primary healthcare and the damage done to patients by fragmented medicine. GPs are heralded as the backbone of the healthcare system and I immediately spotted an opportunity for him to pen a powerful column about his frontline experience. He was well read and measured in speech, so I trusted his ability to write convincingly about a subject he knew well, but he doubted that anyone would read him (the aforementioned 'Who, me?' syndrome).

Professionals can hesitate to engage with the public because they feel that their opinions are not valued or that they risk exposing themselves to criticism or backlash. While this can happen, in this instance the doctor's concerns were unfounded. Predictably, a younger doctor wrote an impassioned column on the same topic. It was featured on the front page of a national newspaper, sparking an important conversation and giving the writer a foot in the door of writing for the public.

Here are some questions that all aspiring writers should ask themselves.

What is interesting about my work?

Unlike most modern-day workers, I have worked in one job, in the public hospital system, for 25 years. I have risen in seniority and added pursuits such as writing, public speaking and board positions, but my core job is that of a doctor. Like any role, it carries significant routine.

But equating routine with being uninteresting would mean parking my imagination and never writing another column about the art of medicine, a subject I find endlessly engrossing for its many facets. So, I make it a point to be curious throughout the day.

I do this by listening closely to my patients; watching how they navigate the demands of modern life through illness; recalling how my practice has changed over the years; reflecting on how being a mother to three children and a daughter to ageing parents influences my thinking; and noting how my own friends and I, once young and carefree, have come to an age where we are having to grapple with our own illnesses and mortality. This alone provides enough material for years' worth of reflection, opinion and advocacy.

To write well, never underestimate the value of simple observation.

What makes you stop and think? What conversations are your neighbours and friends having? What are your colleagues discussing? What political or social issues occupy your organisation's energy?

What evidence and knowledge do I have to inform a column?

The problem with evidence is just how much of it there is. Over 5 million academic papers on all kinds of topics are published each year; I feel defeated just thinking about the few journals I want to read every week. But lived experience and distilled knowledge are valuable, too, and in doing the kind of writing I do, I find this thinking more useful.

I don't know a good writer who is not an avid reader. For ideas and inspiration to inform my columns, I read newspapers including *The Age* (for Australian news and current affairs, health policy and healthcare utilisation), the *Guardian* (Australian and international perspectives), the *New York Times*, the *New Yorker* and the *Economist* (for exceptional writing on a wide range of topics including books, current events and science, not to mention fine obituaries).

I subscribe to a handful of medical journals, such as oncology publications and the *New England Journal of Medicine*, to keep pace with medical advances and skim the free contents list of some other journals that land in my inbox. Finally, I am never without a work of fiction at my bedside table even though I am a slow reader and am learning to accept that I will never read all the great books I would like.

My reading portfolio appears more daunting than it is. I don't read every publication every week, neither do I absorb or retain as much as I'd like, but I deeply believe that the habit of reading itself is important. Reading stills me, focuses my mind, introduces me to new ideas and inspires me to write as well as the writers I admire.

I fondly remember that while my childhood in India lacked many civic and infrastructure amenities that my parents did not have control over, my brother and I grew up with a treasury of books and magazines. We received multiple newspapers and current affairs magazines and even subscription-only journals (albeit a month or two late) when no one in our circle had even heard of such things.

From a young age, reading widely exposed me to different styles and helped me figure out what I liked and why. From my earliest days of reading, I was drawn to narratives, particularly those written in an easy, conversational style. The best writing transported me to a place where I felt the writer was talking to me at my kitchen table. Even today, my favourite room in the house is my library, where I love being surrounded by the books which silently stand guard around me.

Today, my goal is to take seemingly routine topics (for instance, aged care funding, hospital overcrowding, healthcare resourcing, end-of-life care, substance abuse, frailty, obesity) and illustrate their significance through storytelling. If you humanise the evidence, you will engage readers.

Who is my audience and how might my readers benefit from my input?

In writing for an audience, it is important to know who constitutes that audience.

When writing, I like to imagine that I am speaking to a person. The person reading my *Guardian* column is typically middle-aged, well educated, professional, left-leaning and knowledgeable about government, policy and current affairs. A more recent group of my readers comprises healthcare students, trainees and young doctors. I envisage my audience as curious, reflective, and interested in sharing my work with like-minded people or those who might have something to learn from my reflections. Over the last ten years, as I have begun to meet the people who read me, I think this accurately sums them up.

Recently, a terminally ill patient wrote to me to say that her friend, a *Guardian* reader, pointed her to my books and columns because the patient is frustrated with her voice not being heard amidst the upset and mayhem of navigating cancer. She was writing to thank me because she found both consolation and practical help from my writing. The knowledge that my readers gain something from my writing that they want to amplify felt like a wonderful 'side effect'.

On the other hand, my reader is not the patient I frequently encounter in my cancer clinic – a vulnerable refugee or migrant, non-English speaking, with a primary school education or less, lost in the healthcare maze, who has never even heard of the *Guardian*. While this is the person I would most like to help, it won't be directly through my writing.

But my writing can help them indirectly through raising awareness of and advocating for their needs.

First, the act of writing about medicine helps me think clearly and reflect on people's priorities, which makes me a more deliberate physician. Second, when policymakers read them, my columns can be a source of informal advocacy. Indeed, one of the best pieces of career advice a senior bureaucrat gave me is that, given my interests, I was best placed to influence change through writing. My public profile sometimes allows me easier access to academia, government and industry that I can use, and have used, to give voice to the concerns of my patients.

How could writing a column help me achieve my personal or professional goals?

Being honest, showing vulnerability, demonstrating insight and, where required, professional expertise, are for me, the hallmarks of good writing. This kind of writing needs time. Whether you are writing one opinion or advocacy piece or hope to make a career of writing, it is important to ask why.

Is it to differentiate yourself from your peers? Is clear written expression a step on the ladder to your success? Or, like many people, you might just want to feed a creative urge or get something off your chest.

More than thirty years since I entered medical school, I am still conscious and grateful that my medical education was taxpayer funded. Without this gift, I may not have been able to fulfil my ambition of becoming a doctor. So, upon graduating, I pledged to dedicate myself to the public hospital system. For me, writing is an extension of this service to society, especially to all the people who are never going to be my patients but nevertheless could benefit from my education and training.

The more years I spent as a doctor, the more I was excited by the reach of modern medicine, but I also felt bothered about the fragmentation of care, deficient doctor–patient communication, and ethical dilemmas that did not get the attention they deserved. Tired of appealing to the profession, I thought that engaging the public was another way of influencing change. After all, the public was our customer.

Since I was a jittery columnist with little expectation of success, today I am surprised that my books and columns are used as teaching tools and I am frequently invited to give talks on the art of medicine. For me, writing was a tool to help me process my jumbled thoughts and keep up the process of calibrating myself to be a better oncologist. That it has led to public recognition is a nice postscript.

Once you have found your topic, interrogate it

Once I have found a topic, I am eager to explore it, but I recommend a final cautionary step – interrogating the topic. Questions that have saved me include:

- Is this an evolving issue (such as an ongoing court case)? Writing about an impending court case could jeopardise the outcome, a heavy burden for many, including the writer.
- Does this column require nuanced information I don't (yet) have? I have been caught short more than once by being too eager to write without having all the facts at hand.
- Could my column harm someone, either by disclosing sensitive information or damaging their reputation? I find no column worth writing if it hurts someone.
- Are there parties who might object to my column and what might they say? This generally does not dissuade me from writing; rather, it helps me consider how to address opposing viewpoints.

- What is the worst-case scenario if I write this column, and am I prepared to handle criticism? This also doesn't stop me from writing but does inject pause for thought.

Thinking about these questions, asking someone if not sure, and exercising judgement and discretion help limit fallout and regret from writing. I don't always get it right and lean on my editor (and sometimes, the legal team). However, a check list that helps me focus on possible unwanted outcomes is useful.

Finally, there are occasions when an idea is important, but the timing is not right.

Once, I met a thoughtful first-year teacher frustrated by the lack of support for special-needs students. She complained that the school administrators were out of touch with reality and wanted to call them out. I saw the potential for her lived experience to inform a compelling column but also shared her concern about possible repercussions from her employer. I also thought she made a good point wondering if, as a new teacher, she understood all the nuances of the issue.

Teachers are a trusted voice in society and their perspectives shape public opinion. The sobering experience of a new teacher would make a convincing contribution to a longstanding and complex issue, but she was prudent to consider the risks. Being on a temporary contract, she didn't want to jeopardise her chances of permanent employment and decided to keep talking to advocacy groups to learn more.

This is an example of making judicious decisions based on personal circumstances and a thoughtful consideration of the potential downsides of writing for the public.

It is also why I keep a journal where I write all sorts of things that are not ready for public airing. I find this a great way of debriefing, venting and rearranging my thoughts. You could consider this and discover that the habit of keeping notes is preparation for one day writing for the public.

A strong column should bring satisfaction to your readers and you, the writer. Approaching it in a thoughtful and intentional way ensures that it will make an impact.

TIPS
1. It is usually not a lack of ideas but confidence that inhibits writers.
2. Think about relevance, interest and timing.
3. Consider using a checklist to stress-test your idea.

My life became entwined with a stranger in a tense mid-air drama

As a doctor, I have to be prepared to attend to a sick passenger on a flight. I never found out if one particular patient recovered

18 April 2018

Guardian

'If there is a doctor on the flight, please . . .'

The call for a doctor reflexively ejects me out of my seat and towards the sick patient.

One flight in every 600 incurs a medical emergency – until recently I used to pack my trusted stethoscope that could actually hear a thing or two amid the din of the plane, but it felt too much like inviting illness. Leaving my stethoscope behind is the first thing I regret.

In the centre seat is a sallow-looking, slightly built woman who says in soft, accented English that she feels a bit faint. Except she looks terrible.

'I am a doctor, here to help you,' I say.

'Thank God,' she says fervently as her head sinks into the lap of her startled co-passenger, jammed against the window.

'Not yet,' I think grimly, with moments to gather my senses and a history.

She has diabetes and renal failure. She woke up very early for dialysis before boarding the cross-country flight to visit her son. She felt dizzy, no different to usual. But now, hours later, she is sweaty and uncomfortable. I have been groping her wrist the whole time; locating the faint thread of a pulse, I tell the flight attendant to summon help.

Reinforcement arrives in the form of a man in whom I long to find an emergency worker because I suspect the patient is having a silent heart attack.

'I am an oncologist,' is my way of conveying that it's been a long time since I resuscitated something other than a dummy.

'Me too,' he says, almost apologetically. We look at each other in dismay.

Airway, breathing, circulation, I repeat to no one in particular as a sparse medical kit appears. He connects her to oxygen while I rummage for an aspirin, which I can't find.

'Thank you,' she says once, and I can't help but feel moved, and a little scared, by her show of faith in me.

'I think you might be having a heart attack. Do you carry aspirin?'

'I can't have aspirin,' she replies.

Before I can ask why, she is already unconscious.

The blood pressure cuff works but the stethoscope is tinny and useless.

'What do you think?' an anxious attendant asks.

'She might arrest.'

'The captain says we are landing in an hour, do your best.'

A nurse has heard the commotion and has made her way to help. But she doesn't feel confident inserting an IV amid the mild turbulence and I don't blame her.

The patient opens her eyes, allowing the frightened window-seat passenger to scuttle from her seat. To prevent crowding, the other oncologist returns to his seat and the nurse takes a seat across the aisle. I put my mouth close to the patient's ear.

'I know this must feel frightening but I won't leave you.'

I turn my attention to her husband, pale-faced and utterly silent, riven with apprehension and foreboding.

'I didn't know this would happen.'

'You can't predict these things,' I reply.

Having made my promise to the patient, I slide into the window seat and put her head in my lap as she curls against the other two seats. Pretending to read a book, I keep a grip on her elusive pulse. 'Stay with me,' I whisper after every paragraph and she flutters her eyelids in response.

'Thank you,' she says once, and I can't help but feel moved, and a little scared, by her show of faith in me. In this confined space, my knowledge seems useless. Instead, all I have to give is the reassurance of my presence and the comfort of a human touch. My mind scoffs that this isn't enough. My heart says it's better than nothing. Her pulse can't agree, skipping too many beats for my liking. I fake calm with my senses on high alert.

With twenty minutes to land, I lose her pulse, forced to confront the scenario that was only ever meant to be a simulation – a patient without a pulse and me as the first responder. There is a yawning silence before the nurse shouts the blindingly obvious: 'No pulse? Start CPR!'

CPR in a row of economy seats? How? With stricken passengers watching? And a husband who has begun grieving? I clamber awkwardly onto the middle seat, my head hitting the ceiling. And then, miraculously, just as my hands are about to bear down on her chest, the nurse exclaims, 'Wait, I feel a pulse!'

I breathe.

'Doctor,' the attendant whispers conspiratorially. 'We are running out of oxygen.'

The longed-for landing causes my patient to vomit.

'The paramedics are here,' I soothe her, wiping her face.

As she is bundled up, I seize the opportunity to prepare her husband.

'There will be a lot going on, but you are in safe hands.'

He seems unconvinced. Looking as if he is about to lose a tenuous connection, he asks desperately, 'But how will I find you again? How will I let you know?' His genuine gratitude in the midst of palpable fear moves me, although I am aware of how little I have actually done. I want to say that her arriving alive is my reward, but I scribble down some details and hurry him in the direction of the rushing paramedics.

A week passes, then a month and more. I keep hoping for some news but there is no word from him and no medical record for me to quietly look up, as I don't even know her full name. In time, she turns into a rare entity in this hyperconnected world of ours – a complete stranger whose life became entwined with mine in a tense mid-air drama before we parted ways.

The lack of closure goes both ways – I still find myself thinking about the patient when I am about to fly and console myself with the old adage, no news is good news, while I ponder whether or not to pack my stethoscope.

About this column

My heart still thumps reading this column, which was nominated as part of a trio for the Walkley Award for Excellence in Journalism, Australia's most prestigious journalism award. Years later, I remember exactly where I was and how I felt when this incident took place and still think about the poor patient and her husband.

Finding a Topic

It didn't take me long to realise that this intense experience would be a perfect topic to write about, and simultaneously debrief myself. A lot of things had happened very fast during the flight and I needed to debrief before boarding the long-haul leg back to Melbourne. Reliving the experience through writing was one way of exorcising my thoughts. The drama of the situation needed no embellishment, no research and no second-guessing; an honest rendition would do. I remember finding a free computer terminal in the lounge and typing out the first draft without pause.

I couldn't help but wonder if publishing this raw column made me appear useless or, worse, incapable. Indeed, a few people said as much, but the truth is that even emergency professionals would struggle to provide urgent care in cramped conditions, so I was telling it like it was and being vulnerable. For me, the real story was not the medical emergency but the importance of humanity when everything else felt impossible.

Many wonderful comments vindicated me. I was buoyed by the reader who called my writing 'the best, most human, yet scientific stories', for bridging the gap between the science and art of medicine because this is always my aim. And I was deeply touched by an anonymous doctor who recalled working with me and finding me 'compassionate and insightful'. No one writes for these rewards, but they undeniably lift morale and provide a basis for keeping going during times of drought and doubt.

3

Who Am I Writing For?

'I write to discover what I know.'
Flannery O'Connor

Even though I love to write, I still go through phases, especially during hectic professional or personal times, when my motivation wilts. Writing requires a lot of time and headspace. Sometimes, chased by a deadline, I delay going home after work and find an empty room at the hospital when I would much rather watch a movie with my boys or talk clothes with my daughter. No family home is complete without a ticker tape of chores like ironing, cooking and cleaning, but writing is a commitment, too.

Sometimes I would like to be a regular writer without having to write regularly. So, I periodically ask myself this question: who am I writing for?

When writing in the *Guardian*, I believe that I write to dignify the experiences of my patients. I also write on behalf of the different people I work with, from niche specialists to mortuary workers, to give voice to our shared experiences of healthcare, uplifting and dejecting. I also write to empower my readers, who are people before being patients. Thinking in this way refuels my sense of purpose.

The next connected question is: how can I give voice to these experiences?

Who Am I Writing For?

Everywhere you look, there are stories to be told. Indeed, life is a series of stories, and people connect through stories. One of my earliest memories is of my mother patiently spooning food into my reluctant mouth while relating Indian fables in a ritual that I'd later adopt with my own children. Telling stories is a compelling way to convey experiences, evoke emotions and communicate effectively with readers.

Let me share two examples.

In an era of fragmented healthcare, my encounters with patients leave a deep mark and often test my hopes of doing better. A common sight in hospitals is of frail and elderly patients suffering dementia, who become unsettled in a new environment. Their rhythm and equilibrium are easily disrupted by unfamiliar staff peppering them with questions. The needs of such patients would be better served within their residential facility but systemic problems and unrealistic expectations from family members create a revolving door into the hospital at a high cost to the patient and society.

A second disheartening observation is the widespread use of futile chemotherapy at the end of life. These so-called 'Hail Mary' treatments result in tremendous suffering and cost for patients and providers, particularly for the nurses who must action the questionable decisions of oncologists like me.

I am not alone in being bothered by these experiences, but as a writer, I will willingly harness them (sometimes at the risk of alienating some of my colleagues) to dissect these issues and press for change. Our firsthand accounts hold valuable insights that can shed light on an issue in a personal and meaningful way, which is much more impactful than a statement of dry facts.

Similarly, you can examine events in your own life and profession to inform the bigger picture of your writing. Whether your subject is finance, education, climate, healthcare or another, consider how you can humanise your work to spark empathy and connection.

Writing as a bridge between the personal and public

I think of my columns as a bridge between personal experience and public understanding. *Here is what I see, here is why you should care.*

This helps me use a mix of personal observation and evidence to create a narrative. In this way, I use the power of storytelling and leverage my professional standing to make my writing approachable. But any time I draw on the stories of my patients, my foremost concern is their privacy. I will return to this.

My time as a *Guardian* columnist has continued longer than I had ever imagined – and while I was always happy writing for myself (and, indeed, never stopped), it is a tremendous privilege to write for the public. Like medicine, I regard writing as a form of service to society and have sought to apply my social conscience to column-writing. I work in a highly disadvantaged area that sees large numbers of migrants, refugees and asylum seekers struggle to access healthcare and other societal goods. As an oncologist, I am in the room with the decisions, dilemmas and difficulties faced by almost everyone at the end of life. I find that I write best when I reflect on real-life experiences and illustrate them with my observations and, where warranted, expert advice.

I have written about unexpected deaths when patients are not properly heard, lack of civic infrastructure like transport and absent social supports as a root cause of missed healthcare, and language and cultural barriers causing costly misunderstandings. Rather than feeling privately exasperated, I use writing as a vehicle to help readers, other health professionals and decision-makers appreciate societal issues that not everyone necessarily encounters. This form of advocacy feels especially satisfying when, in an era of instant communication, a column published in one country can find a receptive audience around the world.

As an example, after a sabbatical at the University of Chicago, I established a hospital service dedicated to elderly cancer patients whose care requires an especially thoughtful approach. Patients who develop cancer while suffering from conditions such as dementia, organ failure and frailty merit explicit discussions about whether the risk of aggressive treatments outweighs the potential benefit and their wishes around the end of life. Unfortunately, these conversations don't happen nearly as often as they ought to, which is what made the holistic objective of my clinic greatly satisfying. But while my patients appreciated its focus, I couldn't escape the feeling that progress was slow and that convincing other professionals to embrace change was hard work.

Writing about the practical outcomes and many ethical dilemmas emerging from this clinic has helped me to communicate directly with the public and empower healthcare consumers to become their own best advocates. My aim is to equip them with the knowledge and tools to ask the right questions to receive the quality of care they merit.

I often think that even if a few hundred people read my column and just a fraction of them learn something valuable, it will surpass the impact I could make from changing outcomes one patient at a time. Therefore, it is both astonishing and gratifying when thousands of readers end up reading, refining and spreading my messages.

I have discovered that one or two powerful columns can eclipse a lifetime of one-on-one conversations.

Embrace storytelling

I remember being a young oncologist and writing a grant proposal, cringing at my boss's admonition to 'ditch the storytelling and stress the data'. She was right but it was the opposite of what I loved doing. I persevered, didn't receive the grant and hated the process. A few more tries put paid to the idea of being an academic researcher who wrote grants to get by.

Academic writing is important – I know how much I rely on it to treat my patients. But it's not right for me and I am glad I had the courage to admit it, otherwise I might have been a dejected researcher.

But writing an engaging column for the public fulfils my idea of a challenge. Instead of blandly stating facts and figures, I come alive at interpreting them through the lens of a narrative.

For instance, the high rate of youth unemployment and its associated problems can be highlighted by painting a vivid picture of a young person sleeping rough and exposed to the temptations and the dangers of street crime. The grim statistics of childhood malnutrition are powerfully illustrated by a description of a toddler delayed in achieving every milestone, with lifelong consequences. There are many ways of depicting the opioid crisis, but nothing brings it home for me like the story of the patient whose life was marred after he was first prescribed unnecessary opioids in the emergency department of a hospital after sustaining a simple injury.

Being bold and authentic in your descriptions engages the senses, allowing the reader to build an emotional connection with your work. Good writing answers my high school English teacher's call to *'put me there'*.

It's helpful to remember that the stories may be universal, but you are telling them in a way only you can tell. Getting the balance right between presenting the facts and engaging the reader is the ultimate joy of writing for the public.

TIPS

1. Good writing harnesses facts into relatable stories.
2. Find the right balance between evidence and anecdote.
3. Use bold and authentic descriptions to capture the imagination.

My young cancer patient refused all treatment. After her death I found out why.

The premature loss of a cancer patient is something that is anathema to an oncologist. Could I have done more to change her mind?

22 November 2023

Guardian

'Every time I talk to you, I feel more distressed.'

Tears stream down the patient's face as she claps her palms over both ears to shut me out.

I am stunned to my core by this completely unexpected office version of a devastating domestic diatribe from which you wonder how you will recover. In my small office, the distance between us feels suddenly uncrossable.

This is our umpteenth meeting. When she was first diagnosed with cancer, she faced a brutal series of treatments. Chemotherapy felled her. Radiation burnt her. The constant needle pricks coloured her skin black and blue. She hated the rumbling noise of the scanner. Yet she persevered because a cure was within reach. The unfortunate problem with many cancers, of course, is that when 'everything is over' it is not always over. Being diagnosed in the first half of one's life leaves the second half to a recurrence. This is what happens some years later during routine surveillance.

Bracing myself, I prepare her for the bad news. I acknowledge her past difficulties to show her how well I recall them. Then I say that while the news is disappointing, this cancer, too, is curable – and thanks to new developments, the treatment will be less onerous. Like many patients, all she hears is that she has cancer. Again.

When she declares this can't be possible, I respond with a respectful silence, knowing that most patients get past the early shock and ask what next. She walks out, perplexed but not ready to let me in.

The next series of consults prove trying for us both. She expresses more surprise than dismay, more curiosity than urgency. My consternation grows but it never crosses my mind that she will refuse curative treatment.

I believe in patient autonomy and am comfortable with the notion of patients refusing treatment where survival gain is minimal or bought at the cost of 'time toxicity', where patients spend the end phase of life shuttling between infusion centres and tests.

In the geriatric oncology service I run, much of my time is spent reassuring my oldest cancer patients that less is more. But this patient is in her forties with a curable illness, so the usual rules don't apply.

Today, she has arrived hours early so she can 'dispense' with me before collecting her children from school. I ask her how she is, and she says fine. I fret it's not for long.

I ask when she will have treatment and she says never. My reaction must be painted across my face. When I explore her decision, she says that her greatest wish is to be around for her children. She wants to work, pay the mortgage and support her husband in raising a family. Listening to her, I find her goal poignant, admirable and, given the biology of her cancer, unattainable without treatment.

Doctors are routinely taught, even hectored, to respect patient choice, but given the glaring discordance between what she wishes and what I know will happen, I feel obliged to name my fear.

'But don't you see that the way to be around for your children is to have some treatment? How will you earn an income if you can't work? How will you help your husband if you are unwell?'

This is when she bursts into tears, accusing me of multiplying her distress. But even as she castigates me, I can smell her desperation as she can smell mine. Try as we might, we can't find a compromise. Watching her leave the room, I am flooded with the most abject feeling of loss.

She subsequently forgoes appointments and declines calls and texts, but when I want to discharge her from my clinic, a nurse gently suggests I leave the door open. Enter another wave of guilt and self-doubt at the missed opportunity for cure. The inevitable happens – she presents with an emergency. Hope raises its head; I am thrilled when she returns to see me. Our conversation is calm but my appeal is denied. Again, she forgoes a chance of prolonging survival.

Other emergencies follow. Then, she dies. All this I learn through morsels of third-party information, an unsettling thing when your entire job is in the 'helping industry'.

The oncologist's tonic is closure. Without it, the ghost of one event always threatens to intrude into the next – and at least I think it impacts patient care. Every few months, I try to call her husband.

Much time passes before we connect. From his tone, it's clear I am not the only one searching for closure. There is a workplace grieving initiative, but he knows that the journey of grief is largely undertaken alone, in one's own time.

Eventually we get to a point where I hope for the great reveal. Why did my patient refuse curative treatment?

'She believed that her previous suffering would be rewarded by a lifetime cure.'

He goes on to explain her unshakeable belief that she had done enough the first time round and it did not make sense to have cancer again. Her will to shield her family was so strong it overtook her fears about herself. The longer she deferred treatment, the more she was convinced it was unnecessary. We talk some more about her thoughts and beliefs that we will never know for sure. Finally, he consoles me not to feel badly because I did nothing wrong.

My vindication is tinged with humility. All this time, I had attributed her reluctance to a mixture of wild alternative therapies, mistrust of hospitals and misgivings about my care. Now I can't help wondering whether things could have been different had she trusted me enough to divulge her belief.

Patients who refuse curative treatment often do so based on their values, while their flummoxed doctors act from a place of rationalism.

Could I have met her expectation of some divine benediction with my grounding in science? How would I have pitted her hope against my chemo? I like to think that I would have listened and negotiated but I bet the reason she didn't return is because she feared judgment.

In conventional medicine, the premature loss of a cancer patient marks a missed opportunity for a cure, something that is anathema to an oncologist. But I can't help thinking that in this instance, the greatest loss was the premature loss of understanding.

About this column
Since the time it occurred, this incident never stopped haunting me.

Maybe it was a confessional to process my own disappointment at how badly things had gone, not only the circumstances of my patient's death but also the preceding events that were upsetting.

But I hoped that the column was not entirely self-serving, because after I spoke to the patient's husband, I felt a sense of unfinished business, as if he sought redemption, and she, understanding. Our conversation prompted me, with his consent, to highlight the rift between how patients experience illness and how doctors intellectualise it, a recurring theme of my writing.

I was surprised that a piece describing a not-so-extraordinary occurrence in my work would touch a raw nerve around the world and become a fevered discussion point.

The flip side of a popular column is that it inevitably attracts judgement and, with it, some stinging commentary. Being labelled obnoxious, insincere, arrogant, tone-deaf, inappropriate and unprofessional is never nice – to be considered all this in a space of a day is particularly hard. For a viscerally felt piece to be denounced as 'creative writing' felt like a double blow. And these were the comments that made the moderators' cut.

On the other hand, many readers and health professionals offered enlightened comments and advice that enhanced my understanding of the experience of illness and helped me during future conversations with patients. You can read the comments online.

Upon reading some of the more scorching comments, a concerned friend asked how I had the stomach to 'do this' every fortnight since she felt riled on my behalf after spending just a little time on the site. But to take only the criticism to heart and ignore the wisdom would be to do an injustice to reader contribution.

Constant praise would dilute its novelty, and moreover, I would worry about being predictable and, hence, not growing as a writer. This is why I ask my editors to open comments on every column I write (although sometimes, due to a shortage of moderators, they don't).

It is essential to be true to yourself when writing.

I had been honest and introspective in this column even if it didn't land well with everyone. Not seeking audience approval meant that neither the criticism nor the praise felt personal.

When a column has been controversial, I like to ask myself if, given a second chance, I would write the same column again. In this case, I would.

4

How to Build a Column

> 'You must take your readers into the story as if you were telling it to them around a campfire.'
> Ralph Waldo Emerson

Despite years of writing, or perhaps because of it, I still worry about how to turn a good idea into a readable column. Maybe it's because I have experienced many ways in which the process can be derailed: from inattention to detail to aiming for perfection, and from being underqualified to straying into overconfidence.

But for ideas to enter the public discourse, they must be expressed. And even though a part of me wonders how, the sheer idea of wrestling a big topic into a 900-word column energises me.

Some days, my words flow effortlessly because the idea and its associations work. On other days my thoughts jangle without outcome. When you have a job that demands your full attention and writing is not your main gig, good writing can seem unreachable.

In the week my column is due, I often attend clinic fantasising that there will be time to ponder a column. Mostly, morning blends into evening without any such thing happening, but I go home with the temptation of using the next day to build a column from scratch.

Organising thoughts out of chaos

A column asks that we move, inform and convert the reader with a tight set of words. We have all read books that leave us craving a less forgiving editor but column writing especially rejects padding and must be on point.

When writing an advocacy piece, for instance, there is a natural tendency to pile on arguments, hoping that a parade of compelling points will sway the reader. But I like to think of writing a good column like cooking a favourite dish: resisting the urge for excess or embellishment, instead selecting ingredients for balance and depth. As someone drawn to 'big' words, long sentences and fed on a fair amount of inscrutable academic text, it has taken me a very long time to appreciate what charm there is in simplicity.

Take time to mull your topic over and do some basic research. You might need to lean on evidence and statistics but, wherever possible, insert a human angle because stories stay with us so much longer than facts. I can't count the times this small but vital preliminary work has helped me decide my 'statement of belief', or the nub of my column.

Structure

Early on in writing, I envisage my thesis as one of the following:

'This is in the public interest because . . .'

'We might all learn something from this because . . .'

'I have this perspective because . . .'

This starting point gives structure to my writing and helps me move from beginning to middle to end. Here is an example.

I recently read a medical journal article about the remarkable benefits of exercise on cancer survival, the idea being that even a small amount of exercise, especially those that shift a person from sedentary to modest activity, is helpful in prolonging survival. This is an important finding because cancer treatment takes such a toll that people can't fathom the idea of exercise. But they might be encouraged to know that even half an hour of exercise can be life changing.

The problem with much good research is that it's tucked away behind a paywall. When I read the article, and thought about my patients, I knew I had to share these findings with the public.

My thesis was straightforward: 'Every cancer patient should know the link between exercise and improved survival.'

But how to build a column to provide just the right amount of understanding for a general audience? My next task was to comb the data and identify the most relevant parts of the article. Again, I thought of my readers as curious and engaged people seeking exposure to new ideas without necessarily wanting to become experts.

This helped me build the following structure: what the evidence stated, how much exercise was enough, what benefits might accrue, and where to begin. I thought about my own patients to come up with a 'composite' person who represented the potential beneficiary of these findings.

What did I leave out? The kind of minute detail about physiology and fitness measurements that would be valuable to someone wanting to replicate the academic study but not relevant to the casual reader.

Imagine dividing your column into five roughly equal paragraphs – one introductory, three in the middle, and one concluding.

The opening paragraph contains the hook, the idea that draws the reader to the column. This is where I use the news, an event or an experience as a launching pad. You can try experimenting with an anecdote, quote or question that invites further reading.

Use the middle paragraphs to make two strong points but no more than three. A column is diluted by including too many ideas or those that are not worked through satisfactorily. Put yourself in the reader's shoes to appreciate the cognitive load of leaping across too many ideas in the space of a relatively short piece. And remember, if you have more to say than can fit into a column, you can always consider a different form of writing such a feature article.

I like to stress test my own work by asking the following questions:

- Which arguments will strengthen my column?
- Which claims should be backed by credible references?
- What personal experiences and insights can I bring?

Apart from clearly setting out a point of view, a good column makes a point of considering different perspectives, anticipating and pre-emptively addressing opposition. I find these aspects of writing some of the most enjoyable and challenging as a writer.

What was the last piece you read that made you think? Perhaps you ended it feeling grateful, reflective or educated for having a better grasp of an issue that you didn't even know you cared about. Maybe, like me, you enhanced your contentment by sending it to like-minded friends.

This is the gift of a column that ends well. Finishing on a memorable note is a call to savour the writing all over again. I love discovering good writing and get renewed pleasure out of sending it to my friends who might agree despite our varied interests.

Stop planning and start writing

There is an adage: how do you eat an elephant? Bite by bite. It's one that I regularly use as self-encouragement because to become a writer is to stop planning and start writing.

I encourage you to begin by writing one paragraph at a time without worrying about how they will fit together.

Each point you make can serve as a natural stop and a motivation to continue before tackling organisation and flow. It's important to stick to a rough word limit otherwise the task of editing becomes unwieldy. As mentioned earlier, for a 900-word column, I aim to stop at 1,000 words and have a hard stop at 1,100. Anything more wastes too much time to cut back.

Following these tips will get you to a first draft. Then I am a fan of putting it aside. Sleeping on a column is one of the best ways to improve your writing. You may have a short deadline but if possible, leave yourself time to read your work two or three times. Then, rejecting the temptation of making endless tweaks without adding value, press send.

The writer Roald Dahl observed that good writing is essentially repetitive writing. He is said to have put his work through at least 150 edits, being suspicious of both facility and speed.

Roald Dahl suffered through many more edits than me but if you pair his point with the notion that all good writing (still) leaves something unexpressed, you have yourself a start.

My editor and I might exchange clarifications and minor edits but, once filed, I take two days of complete mental break before turning my mind to the next column. I should add that well before becoming a columnist with a deadline, I was taught by a wonderful medical school professor and writing mentor, who told me to 'always be writing something'. Like a lot of good advice, it was pithy, sound and continually useful.

TIPS

1. Having a short, clear thesis in mind will help structure your writing.
2. Make a column manageable by dividing it into four or five sections.
3. Two or three well-made points are better than several weak ones.
4. To improve quality, rest your draft and mind.

When I delivered the worst of news to my dying patient, she cried – but not about her prognosis

We like to think patients judge us for our medical acumen but, in fact, they observe the words we say, the empathy we show and the kindness we offer

23 October 2024

Guardian

'Now I am crying because you are sitting *there*.'

'I am sorry,' I say, preparing to jump up.

'No, please stay!'

This is our first meeting. 'There' is by her feet, tucked to one side of her hospital bed to make room for me. She has been interrogated and prodded by all types of doctors. 'The moment I saw her, I knew she needed you,' the last of her specialists told me.

Oncologists like me aren't flattered by such statements: when called to see a patient at the tail end of an admission, it's to deliver the worst kind of bad news. Or more accurately, to collect the fragments of bad news into a cogent explanation and confirm what everyone has hinted at: the illness is serious and the prognosis grave.

She is a wife, mother and the kind of amicable person one could readily imagine delivering just-baked cookies to a friend or offering to mind a neighbour's baby.

After weeks of investigations for recurrent cancer, she is despondent.

One surgeon places her on the operating list. A second, junior surgeon isn't convinced but holds his tongue. A third surgeon, who was scheduled to perform the operation, cancels it and I see why: while surgery is technically feasible, the most predictable outcome would be to prolong hospitalisation at the risk of wasting what precious time remains of her life.

She has a clear-eyed understanding of her impossible situation but still, filling in the gaps feels punitive. I tell her the surgeon was right to spare her the futile surgery.

We discuss that chemotherapy would be unhelpful. She asks how long, then adds she figures time is short. I touch her arm, swallow and nod.

And then she is crying. The teardrops are plunging from her eyes, sliding down her cheeks and into the back of her sleeve. I look around for tissues; she tearfully jokes that we are in a public hospital.

But here is the thing. She isn't crying because I have just admired her unrivalled poise. She is not even crying about her prognosis or that she won't see the grandchildren growing up.

She is crying, she says, because kindness melts her.

One surgeon sat there, she says with a grimace, pointing to the windowsill. From his perch, he spoke quickly and loudly, telling her she was dying and seemingly wanting the 'whole world' to know. In the middle of speaking, he took a phone call – she had found his blitheness unforgivable.

In contrast, she argues, the junior surgeon was professional *and* kind. He had pulled up a chair and made eye contact. His honesty and warmth were so comforting that she memorised his name. Her eyes light up – as do mine, because it just so happens she is describing my friend.

I first met him when I was trying to talk a dying patient out of surgery but not getting very far. Just then he arrived and, after waiting for me to finish, gently took the man's hand and said, 'If you were my father, I wouldn't want you to have an operation.' His soft tone settled the matter and I remember thinking that if ever there was an example of a healing touch, this was it.

My patient is crying again, and she tells me that now she is crying at the memory of a single incident that will define her stay.

One morning, a bevy of doctors had towered by her bedside. As the boss rained incessant bad news upon her, everyone stood wordlessly and she felt suffocated by fear. Then, at the back of the crowd, she spotted a young man crying – 'and all of a sudden I felt better'.

He returned to introduce himself as the intern, saying how much the bad tidings had affected him. He sat down and talked to her about her health, her children and her shredded hopes. Here was the person with the least agency taking the most time – to her, he had stood out as the best doctor of the lot. (Later, I will find the intern and tell him.)

I am deeply moved but a part of me still can't help thinking the surgeon who cancelled the operation deserves some credit. I offer that he had made the right medical decision but might have felt anxious having a difficult conversation, but my explanation doesn't fly. Not privy to the decisions made behind the scenes, she only saw how she was treated.

Her account underlines an important attitude among patients that is often missed by doctors. We like to think patients judge us for our medical acumen but, in fact, they observe the words we say, the empathy we show and the kindness we offer. This is a lesson as abundantly available as it is hard to absorb.

It illustrates the continuing gap between how doctors and patients view what really matters in medicine. Doctors are trained to think too much and feel too little. Our patients know we think enough but want us to feel more. As technology, machinery and bureaucracy overwhelm us, the essence of good medicine remains an open secret.

Days after we meet, the loose ends are tied and the patient is preparing to go home for the last time. She reassures me that she is leaving with a light heart, which feels impossible under the circumstances but is a testament to her character. She reflects that she will always remember the warmth that I and others showed her. How telling it is that we came nowhere near extending her life and yet her prevailing response is one of gratitude.

The ancient philosopher Seneca knew this when he said: 'People pay the doctor for his trouble; for his kindness they still remain in his debt.'

About this column

As a new columnist, I constantly feared running out of ideas. I can happily confirm that this fear was unfounded. The more I write, the more keenly I notice things to write about.

When I met the patient above, two things struck me. One, her uncommon courage and two, the intern's kindness. I knew immediately that if I was moved by something that I saw far more frequently than most people, my readers would appreciate it too.

The core message of the importance of kindness in medicine needed neither intellectualising nor varnishing, just simple retelling.

It was a joy to watch this column come alive. Most surprising to me was how such a plain account of something that happens many times a day in every hospital garnered nearly half a million readers and a host of warm comments.

While I am ambitious to write soaring pieces, I considered this a rather modest offering. Indeed, to many of my colleagues, this situation was wholly unremarkable. But maybe, that is the point: impactful writing doesn't have to be novel; there is beauty in the ordinary.

5

Crafting a Strong Start

> 'Every writer I know has trouble
> with the first sentence.'
> William Faulkner

Thankfully, even William Faulkner had trouble getting started. Since reader attention in this age is a premium commodity, the challenge of good writing begins with the first sentence. I remember my disconcertment upon learning the granularity with which publications can track reader engagement and thinking there was no place to hide.

Even a great idea doesn't reduce my agony about exactly how to begin, so I can understand how daunting the opening lines can feel to writers who write less regularly. But as I teach my students, planning helps but overplanning hinders.

Reflect on what engages you

I have found that a useful strategy for writing well is to pay attention to writing that engages you and ask why. While a snappy title or an attractive image can draw readers in, what will keep them coming back is substance. Plus, 'clickbait' writing is uninspiring.

When I began writing for the public, I freely emulated the narrative style used by the doctor-writers I admired. When I read them, I felt that I was in the middle of the action they were describing.

Their storytelling stayed with me – and, moved by the immediacy and poignancy of their writing, I adopted this style but used my own experiences and honed my own words.

You control how you begin your piece – with an anecdote, a quote, a question or an assertion – as well as the tone, voice and tense. My students worry how any of their seemingly simple ideas will attract readers, but with method and practice, you can breathe life into all kinds of topics.

The writer Samuel Johnson enthused that reading was such an important part of writing that a man would turn over half a library to write one book. While not quite half a library, I do find myself skimming a surprising number of things in service of one column.

I dip into a number of publications although I wish I could do each of them greater justice. In an earlier chapter I mentioned that I regularly read medical journals to ably do my job as an oncologist, but these journals are also a great source of information for general interest and, hence, column writing. I subscribe to some newspapers and, when in search of a topic, they are my first port of call. Newspapers are full of ideas that serve as a launching pad for a column to which one can add personal insights – from business and finance to education, healthcare and sports, cooking and fashion.

I pay special attention to opinion pieces to learn how other writers convey their ideas. Reading about subjects that I am not qualified to write about is particularly useful as it helps me appreciate different tones and perspectives. Indeed, reading mindfully is good training to become a better writer.

Novels are an excellent way of landing astute insights, observations and memorable turns of phrase that inspire me to write better. Being a slow reader doesn't deter me as I am always curious to see what makes a book sell. Of course, there are entire genres I would like to discover if I had the time, but every reader I know shares this lament. Compared to those of my friends who churn through books, I am the one to fall asleep with an open book on my face, but it's surprising how inculcating a regular habit of reading adds up in the long term.

I hope I have shown you that expanding your reading is a great way to discover new ways of starting a piece of writing. Think about what you read for work and leisure and note down some memorable aspects to enhance your own writing.

'Put me there'

Back to how to start a column.

In a letter to his brother who harboured literary ambitions, the doctor-writer Anton Chekhov advised seizing on small bits of detail to move the reader.

Instead of writing that the moon was shining, he advised, why not evoke a dam of water on which lay the broken neck of a bottle glittering like a bright little star? Chekhov's words in Russian are frequently condensed by writing instructors as,

'Don't tell me the moon is shining; show me the glint of light on broken glass.' This is another way of putting the timeless lesson of my English teacher: 'Put me there.'

I often open my columns with a quote or anecdote to create immediacy and connect with the reader. For instance, 'Doctor, how long have I got?' is more catchy than the passive, 'One day my patient asked about her prognosis,' although they both say the same thing.

My daughter's road accident one Christmas was a jarring moment in my life. When heralding all the people who helped us, there was no better way to paraphrase her chilling words: 'Just tell me, am I going to die?'

Writing in the first person is one way to put people there.

Sometimes, a vivid description helps. In one column addressing the dangers of sedation in the elderly, I described an elderly hospitalised patient, her head held between scraped, bleeding hands. It's unclear how she got there until we discover that she had suffered a fall after receiving unnecessary sedation in hospital.

This is a common and hazardous hospital complication that many people would be unaware of. Writing about it engaged the public in an important health matter.

A strong start is crucial

My editor observes that she receives so many submissions that she can't read beyond the first few lines, or at most a paragraph, before she has to decide whether to accept or reject a pitch. If the author has not clearly made an impression by the end of the first paragraph, then, even if the idea has merit, it will take so much work to get the writing across the line that it's easier to commission someone else to do it. I find this last point instructive because it means that a publisher can like a pitch but find another writer to do it justice.

Some of my own columns would not pass this test, which makes me strive for improvement.

My editor also advises me that my most-read columns are inevitably human stories, which hold attention because people like to know how stories end. I spend a lot of time crafting a strong start.

Still, a strong start must live up to its promise in the rest of the column – and we will discuss how in subsequent chapters.

The key message is to not get caught in perfecting the start. As your writing evolves, the opening lines might change completely. Make time, write something, keep moving.

TIPS
1. Ask yourself why certain writing catches your attention.
2. Good writers are avid readers. Read widely.
3. Don't let perfect be the enemy of a good-enough start.

Abandonment

31 August 2017

New England Journal of Medicine

'Hospice. It's where people go to die,' she says, surprising me with her sudden lucidity.

'And also for symptom management,' I add gently.

'Like my headache,' she notes.

And your homelessness, I think – *the fact that your one-bedroom, upstairs council flat just won't do anymore.*

'I could go home,' she mutters, moving to squeeze my wrist with her good hand and realising that her hemiparesis won't permit her to turn.

Then, just as suddenly as it had appeared, her lucidity vanishes, in its place a confused silence that grows denser by the day as my patient's cerebral edema worsens. Recently, on routine review, I had told her she was well. Exactly a week later, she landed in a distant hospital after having lost her way to the shops and been found collapsed, her grossly abnormal MRI illustrating why. Cancer wraps all around her brain and has crept into every sinus. The ventricles are swollen, the brain squeezed. It's a sheer miracle that she's been asymptomatic all this time, and despite what everyone says, I am convinced that I missed the signs.

The patient's daughter is her tireless advocate. She calls me to complain that countless providers have swung by, but their advice has been conflicting. Suggestions in just the past few days have ranged from strong opioids and rehabilitation to intrathecal chemotherapy.

'My head is spinning,' the daughter protests.

Crafting a Strong Start

'Mine, too,' I admit. Why are there so many doctors involved, and why aren't they talking to each other? What will a dying patient achieve in rehab? Why did it fall to the daughter to inform me? And what can I do for my patient in a faraway hospital where I have no admitting rights?

Suddenly, her needs feel so overwhelming that I find myself looking for a quick exit. 'Listen, you need to demand better explanations from the treating team,' I say, instantly recognising my prescription for what it is – a way of shielding myself from a story destined to end horribly.

Her voice falters. 'I guess there is only so much you can do.'

Regret washes over me. 'Get some sleep,' I say. 'Leave it with me.'

'I knew you'd help,' she sighs.

I cringe at her misplaced confidence. She doesn't suggest that if I had been more vigilant I could have foretold the impending disaster and spared her mother the embarrassment of being found, incontinent, sprawled across a busy bus stop. It takes many calls to locate a doctor, but eventually it proves straightforward to recommend a transfer to hospice for end-of-life care.

The daughter's relief turns to tension, however, on the eve of discharge. 'Will you be there?' she asks, then answers her own question. 'I guess you can't be everywhere.'

True, the hospice is in a different part of town, but I can't bring myself to say that the real reason I can't manage her mother's care is that I feel sucked into a vortex of issues beyond my control. The daughter's estranged and testy father has suddenly reappeared after many years of absence. Her mother is deteriorating, and I am fielding multiple calls to soothe concerns and allay problems that are outside my usual domain. The better side of me values the trust placed in me, but the other side, the jaded side, resists the responsibility inherent in the trust.

Guiltily, I find myself hoping that my patient's plight ends soon but that I am spared the details. I console myself that she is but one of many palliated patients, and I turn my mind to the patients in clinic awaiting important management decisions. But as I have known all along, the distinction feels fake and eventually wears so thin that one night after work, I drive to the hospice, where my patient greets me with such obvious pleasure that my heart cramps. Before falling asleep, she strokes my hand and whispers my name. I am humbled and slightly aghast that there is room for me within her failing cognition.

Her daughter praises the hospice but laments her father's paranoia that 'everyone is killing' her mother by sending her there.

'I know!' she exclaims, struck by an idea. 'Why don't you talk to him?'

'I will let her doctors know – they are very good at this,' I say, desperately keen to avoid the entanglement.

Some nights later, leaving my hospital, I automatically turn toward the hospice, this time driven only by the thought of making my patient smile. She is seated in a wheelchair, fresh from a trip to the luxurious garden. Holding a sprig of her favourite lavender, she smiles absently. She is mute; there is no sign of recognition. In the room are her ex-husband, her daughter, and suffocating tension.

'Doctor, you tell him that I didn't give her diabetes by feeding her ice cream. She has a different kind of diabetes due to her brain problem.'

Disbelievingly, I explain the difference between diabetes

mellitus and diabetes insipidus, nettled that my patient's final days are being held hostage to pointless disputes.

'So she's stuck here for months, just because you say so?' The ex-husband corners me, threateningly.

'She won't be alive for months,' I whisper.

Understanding dawns on his face, another reminder of the importance of hearing those words from the treating oncologist, even if the news has been discussed many times before. At the front desk, I go to write a note, but I realise that there's nothing to say that the hospice team doesn't already know. Just then, an elderly nurse breaks into my reverie.

'It's good you came,' she says. 'Many patients just feel dumped at hospice.'

My face must reflect my surprise at her blunt term because she shrugs, 'They do, they just don't tell you.'

How can anyone feel 'dumped' in this tranquil, respectful place where kindness and respect never feel optional? Here, there are flowers and sunshine and fresh air. Here, families can visit, stay, argue, and grieve and be supported by professionals. No one can feel 'dumped' here, I silently object, but somehow her words put me on edge. Did I recommend hospice because it was easier on my emotions, or right for the patient? What did I relinquish in the process – my day-to-day involvement or a broader duty of care? Will my patient sense my ambivalence, that I can't quite let go but neither can I stay?

A few days later, the daughter calls me. 'Mum died peacefully the day after you saw her and, incredibly, Dad began to come around. She was too young to die, but thank you for all that you did.'

I am engulfed by a huge wave of sadness, and since every word feels like a platitude, all I say is, 'You should be proud of your effort.'

After the funeral, she calls me to obtain a letter for work. I have one chance to ask the question that has been pricking my conscience, though I can't bring myself to use the nurse's terminology.

'Some people feel abandoned in hospice. Do you think your mother ever felt that?'

'Abandoned? Oh god, no!'

My heart soars with relief. I told you so, I quietly and gleefully retort to the nurse. I could have told you that the peripheral involvement of an oncologist is no match for the comforts and consolations of hospice, that advocacy can stretch only so far, that abandonment by the oncologist is a myth, that patients get over the fact that their oncologist can't be everywhere. From here it's short work to convince myself that perhaps my job can end when patients enter hospice, that things will work out even without my exertions.

'But doctor, you know why, don't you?' the daughter continues, with renewed emphasis. I hold my breath for the denunciation. *You passed off her care*, I expect her to say, *but we got better doctors in the end*. But no. Instead, I hear, 'We felt safe because we knew you had our back. Mum knew you'd take care of her no matter what. You were always going to be her oncologist.'

6

From Thinking Clearly to Writing Clearly

> 'The worst thing you can do is write too much.'
> Voltaire

One of my first board positions on a philanthropic organisation came with an interesting remark from its founder, an erudite man with much life experience. When I asked what he thought I could add to his board he remarked that clear writers were clear thinkers. He had read my work and if I could convey an idea concisely through a column, he sought this attribute for his advisory board.

I hadn't put my finger on it in the same way, but he was right – there is a crucial link between clear thinking and clear writing. Training in one enhances your ability in the other.

Dedicating time and effort to 'just sit and think' sounds faintly indulgent, especially when writing is a side pursuit. But I know that without properly sifting through ideas in my head, I will make slow progress at writing. Therefore, for effective writing, contemplation is not a luxury but a prerequisite.

Like many people, my professional life demands close attention, in this case to the needs of my patients. Paperwork and emails have a way of filling up any quiet moments. At home, my children are my priority, then my ageing parents. Finding time to 'be a writer' is a challenge. I am mildly envious of people who seem to switch on their creative faculties once their other jobs are done but, while this idea is alluring (and I suspect nowhere as easy as it sounds), I prize rest. I rely on sound sleep for my daily emotional recalibration.

Thinking time and places

I am endlessly curious about where other writers do their best work. For some, there are writing retreats, a café or a home office. I have no opinion on any of these because I do most of my writing from my bed, followed by some other unconventional places.

When I am not writing from my bed, the gym happens to be one of my favourite thinking places. Here, the rhythmic strokes of a rowing machine or the steady pace of an elliptical help me 'write' a column in my head. On these machines, my thoughts run loose, arranging and rearranging themselves as I stay busy. I think about a topic, the arguments and counterarguments. Of course, it is not possible to do this in any strict sense but, despite the unconventional setting and loud overhead music, it constantly surprises me how many times I leave the gym with a working idea of a column, which is a positive start.

If the idea of going to the gym to compose a piece of writing in your head seems quirky (or even downright punitive!), you could consider the wonderful alternative of taking yourself for a walk.

The Latin phrase *solvitur ambulando* is attributed to the fourth-century BC philosopher, Diogenes. It means 'it is solved by walking'.

Whether it's tuning into birdsong along a nature trail, watching a sky painted by sunset or walking under moonlight, nature does have a wonderful way of helping us curate our jumbled thoughts. No wonder so many writers credit the power of nature to invigorate the mind.

I love to walk our family dog in an off-leash park. While he runs around madly with pleasure, the quiet, unforced time encourages some of my better ideas and more eloquent expressions, which seems apposite not only for writing but also life's conundrums.

My other thinking ground is located in my car, where I have an opportunity to sit still and drive in silence. Switching off the news or music on a familiar route is great for running through writing ideas.

Since my columns are mostly about healthcare and the human condition, there are always difficulties and good tidings from work to ponder. When deciding what to write about, I think fondly of the poet John Keats' letter to his close friend Benjamin Bailey. 'I am certain of nothing but the holiness of the heart's affections and the truth of imagination.'

Could there be a better reminder to write thinkingly and genuinely?

Of course, every bright idea still needs translating into good writing. Wishful thinking is not a writing strategy.

Consequently, I squeeze in writing in all kinds of places: the unoccupied prayer room of the hospital; the gym reception; the train station waiting to pick up my kids; the nursing home parking lot while my mother visits her friend inside. Indeed, these are the places that suit me since they are not engineered and my expectations are modest.

But by far, my favourite place to write happens to be my bed, propped against some pillows, with our dog at my feet.

Ensconced here, I can't see the kitchen, laundry or the list of errands that must wait. There is something soothingly reassuring and familiar about this setting where many of my best ideas have germinated.

With experimenting, you, too, will find your best fit, but to start, you could try these tips.

Free writing exercise

After loosely organising your thoughts, start writing. Set aside a block of time, say 45 minutes, to write continuously, without worrying about grammar, structure or coherence. The author Philip José Farmer, who wrote science fiction and fantasy, called imagination a muscle, claiming that the more he wrote, the bigger it got. He is like every writer I have met who underlines the importance of habit in writing.

If you are a beginner, know that every writer suffers through the process of revising, editing, re-editing only to get to the point of hating the sight of one's own work – all in the name of eventual clarity and coherence. But the free-writing exercise as a start is something many teachers, including my own high-school teacher, recommend for a good reason.

Free writing will move you towards a draft.

Now, what should one do and not do with this early draft? For one, don't hit delete in a fit of exasperation. I have done this, regretted it, managed to retrieve the document – and realised that it really was cringeworthy. I recently unearthed a book-length manuscript that I tucked away years ago after receiving a lukewarm response that I had found humiliating at the time. Re-reading it, I didn't think the writing, or the response, was as bad as I had imagined.

With time, I have realised that impulsive reactions are not conducive to a writing life. Now, instead of deleting drafts, I store them away even if I never look at them again. At worst, they will remain in an unheralded folder but at best, they might one day yield fresh insights.

The writer Dominick Dunne attributed this advice to his editor when he was writing his first book. His editor told him to finish his first draft and then they could talk, helping Dunne to think that even if he wrote it wrong, it was important to finish the first draft. In turn, Dunne dispenses great advice when he says that only when one has a flawed whole does the writer know what to fix.

He is right. It is easier to edit a clunky paragraph than a blank page. I often write discombobulated drafts to later chip away at. I don't have enough time between deadlines to seek feedback, but if you are a beginner, this can be useful at draft stage.

If you can find one or two people who have the time to offer genuine, constructive feedback, take it. But you must be discerning about choosing your earliest readers. I think it's useful to steer clear of extremes – outright praise ('This is amazing') and blunt rejection ('Nothing works'). Usually, the truth lies somewhere in between and an invested early reader will help you see it.

Once I am happy (enough) with my column, my feedback loop at the *Guardian* includes my editor and, occasionally, the legal team to make sure I am on safe ground, for instance if a matter is in court. I invite openness even if it occasionally elicits a 'sorry, this doesn't work' or 'it's not your best writing', especially dejecting when I am nearing a deadline and have a full list of patients to see. But I love that someone cares enough about the quality of my writing to offer such commentary.

I find it extremely useful to put my work aside and sleep on it. Different from sleeping to avoid writing a column in the first place (procrastination), letting a work 'rest in your head' is something I highly recommend.

I never submit a piece of writing if I can sleep on it first. When we rest, our brain continues to process and mull over ideas, subtly refining them in the background. It's not unusual to wake up with a fresh perspective or an inspired phrase. Sometimes I find that my writing is better than I thought and, other times, worse. Don't be in a hurry to expose your draft to the outside if you can help it.

Draft by draft

Here are some important things to keep in mind when finessing each draft.

Accessibility: Writing for the public is to make an idea accessible. Avoid jargon and cliches. 'Use common words to say uncommon things', advised the philosopher Arthur Schopenhauer. This also happens to be my most useful (and necessary) personal reminder – when in doubt, choose the simpler word. Use 'say' over 'articulate', 'collection' over 'repertoire', 'tireless' over 'indefatigable'. Long sentences and convoluted language are irritating and alienating. The time I needed a dictionary to get through a prize-winning novel, I ditched the author – and felt vindicated to hear a friend complain that his next work suffered from the same problem.

Audience: Treat your reader the way you want to be treated. I view my reader as an interested and intelligent companion in a considered dialogue with me (through the comments section and emails). I am prepared to tackle controversial topics while avoiding a polemical or hectoring tone. This is the kind of writing I like to read because it leaves me thinking – hence, it's the kind of writing I aspire to produce.

Connectedness: A good column or advocacy piece should flow from the first paragraph to the last. The first paragraph contains a hook and harks at what's to come. The middle section, the body, should contain two, at most, three points. All ideas need not receive equal weight – some merit more emphasis than others that you can simply touch on to display your awareness of different perspectives. The final paragraph is important. It is the ribbon that ties things together, so end memorably.

Quality: Prize high-quality writing without getting too precious. It's ridiculously easy to get caught up in the trap of endlessly swapping words and moving sentences while making negligible change. I know because I am guilty of it. This is how many of my students get off to a promising start but fail to meet deadlines. I grade enjoyable columns that end abruptly, sometimes mid-sentence, because the writer ran out of steam. You will know there is no single definition of perfection – just think of all the feted books and essays one reads only to wonder what the fuss is about. At some point, you should accept (or get help to appreciate) that a piece of work is complete and channel your energies towards new projects.

Of course, it would fall to a polymath like Leonardo da Vinci, the artist who painted the *Mona Lisa* and made groundbreaking sketches of the human anatomy, to say that simplicity was the ultimate sophistication.

My final advice is that good writing doesn't need to flaunt itself; its power lies in its simplicity and emotional resonance.

Readers who feel respected will respond to your work. The community created through thoughtful and engaged comments about my columns is a gift for generating more ideas for future writing. Incidentally, this is why I ask my editors to open all my columns to comments and especially ones deemed controversial. (Sometimes comments are closed due to the potential for trolling and a lack of moderators.)

The great thing about writing for the public is gaining the chance to listen to the public.

The journey from a rough draft to a polished piece is challenging and rewarding, but most of all, it is iterative. To write well, be prepared to persevere. And when the job is done, take some time to savour the result.

TIPS

1. Give free writing a try.
2. There is power in simplicity.
3. Sleep on your draft.
4. Don't overthink it.

When is it time for an older doctor to hang up their stethoscope? We owe it to our patients to get it right

A doctor's ability to provide sound patient care diminishes with age. We need a comprehensive, fair and respectful way of assessing fitness to practice

9 October 2024

Guardian

At my medical graduation over 25 years ago, the earnest guest speaker made us promise we would get ourselves a GP. All 160 of us humoured him, secretly believing illness was something that happened to other people.

I was 23 years old then. It took me twenty years to honour the promise. In that time, no friend issued me a prescription or arranged any tests; I guess I was lucky. During pregnancy, my obstetrician took charge but didn't mention getting a GP. Becoming a parent made me realise the importance of objectivity in healthcare, which is how my family found a GP. To be clear, I don't recommend any doctor delay finding a GP like I did, especially in this environment of stress and burnout.

Doctors make poor patients. We self-diagnose, self-refer and ignore symptoms we would never ignore in our patients. We are reluctant to seek care due to a mix of overconfidence, stigma and concerns about gossip and professional viability.

But just like everyone else, older doctors have rising health needs. Even with their greater experience, ageing results in a decline in processing speed, problem-solving ability, dexterity, vision and hearing. Experts advise that first to go is strength, then eyesight, dexterity, and finally, cognition. Knowledge, experience and reputation can compensate for years.

Of the 132,000 practising doctors in Australia, nearly 7,000 (5%) are aged 70 and over. Older doctors are more likely than their younger colleagues to attract complaints about clinical care, communication, record-keeping and prescribing, although it's important to note the absolute difference is small: in 2023, for every 1,000 doctors there were 69 complaints in the over-70 group and 38 in the under-70. Regulatory action occurred in 23% of complaints in the first group and 14% in the second.

The effect of age alone on any individual doctor's competence is highly variable but there is good evidence that on average, doctors' ability to provide sound patient care diminishes with age. When reduced ability is accompanied by reduced insight, seemingly small errors can cause significant harm and death.

Dealing sensitively with doctors while protecting vulnerable patients is the needle that the Medical Board of Australia hopes to thread with its consultation paper.

Three policy options are being considered to ensure late-career doctors are fit to practise.

The first is to rely on the current code of conduct, which expects doctors to have their own GP and be aware of the risks of self-diagnosis and self-treatment. But nudges towards education and independent health advice have not shifted the dial, leading to 'overwhelming support' from stakeholders (including specialist colleges, indemnity providers and consumer groups) for late-career doctors to have a health check that includes some form of cognitive assessment.

This brings us to the second option of a detailed assessment of 'fitness to practice' conducted once every three years after age 70 and annually after age 80. The results and any intervention would be confidential unless the doctor posed a substantial risk to the public.

Such assessments can take up to four hours and cost up to $6,000. Three thousand doctors would be eligible (placing the economic cost at up to $20m per year), but with fewer than 300 occupational health experts to conduct them, the workforce demand would go unmet.

There are other considerations, too. Some doctors may be impaired, but others may find the process onerous enough to retire prematurely, which would particularly impact areas of shortage.

Older doctors can be superb mentors – it would be a shame if regulatory overreach lost them. So, while one might intuitively think the best way to protect the public from impaired doctors is the most detailed assessment, just like in the practice of medicine, the benefits must be weighed against the risks.

Which brings us to the third option: requiring late-career doctors to undergo a general health check that can be completed by the doctor's regular GP or another professional. Many doctors already undergo such health checks, so the economic cost is expected to be up to $2.6m a year.

Active management of doctors' health would serve the public interest in two ways: it would maintain public confidence and it would help other doctors who quietly protect patients from an impaired colleague. Many of us know the dilemma and heartache of knowing that a dear friend is no longer someone we would want treating our loved ones.

Doctors are often compared to judges and pilots because all three make important and consequential decisions.

In Australia, high court and federal court judges must retire at age 70. Pilots must undergo a six-monthly health check after age 60 and a major examination annually.

Doctors enjoy much societal respect and professional autonomy. It's been a long time since I had to 'prove' anything to a regulatory body. I love patient care, strive to stay current and take pride in my judgement. When something goes wrong, my conscience gives me more grief than any authority.

In this, I am no different to nearly every doctor I have known including, unfortunately, those doctors who have grown impaired before my eyes. When they accepted the message they initially resisted – and retired – they, their patients and colleagues were better off.

When it comes to late-career doctors experiencing impairment, what is often missing from the medical establishment is a genuine culture of openness that invites self-awareness, flexible roles and gradual transitions. Instead of being checkbox exercises, performance reviews must include real-world insights from other doctors, nurses, allied health and patients to properly gauge a doctor's competence.

We need a comprehensive, fair and respectful way of assessing older doctors. Will doctors find the board's proposal poisonous or a bitter but necessary pill to swallow? How about the patients who trust us with their lives?

Given the absolute importance of public confidence in healthcare, this is a matter that we should all have a say in.

About this column

I sometimes find good writing ideas from email updates sent by professional bodies. It was while skimming an email between patients that I discovered that the Medical Board of Australia, the regulatory body for doctors, was canvassing submissions on health assessments for older doctors.

Having witnessed impaired doctors during my career, and the excruciating difficulty of telling them that they were not safe to treat patients, the idea of some form of assessment for fitness to practice resonated with me. So, my thesis was simply, 'It's in the public interest to be treated by a competent and healthy doctor.'

Next, I read the Medical Board's consultation paper, 93 interesting pages long. I read it once for my own education and twice more with an eye for the main points to use in a column.

To my initial dismay, there was enough good material for a long-form piece. For instance, I could focus on the types of mistakes made by doctors and sort them by age and country of training. I could also write an interesting piece on why surgeons found it particularly difficult to retire as their identify is more strongly tied to their work. Another topic to explore could be the reasons behind the poor health of many doctors.

Daunted by the task of fitting nearly 100 pages of material into 900 words, I thought of Mark Twain's oft-quoted apology to his friend that if he had more time, he would have written a shorter letter. Column writing forces you to curb your enthusiasm.

I needed to talk myself out of discouragement and read the report and some of its references a couple more times before deciding that my column would discuss the three options outlined by the Board.

When writing about medicine, I take care to not unnecessarily alienate my profession. This is why I conceded up front that for the first forty years of my life, I didn't have a GP, showing (not telling) that doctors make bad patients. This eased my introduction to the Board's options for assessing doctors. The consultation paper went into depth about the different kinds of assessment; here is where I used my judgement to cover the gist. Distilling the substance and shedding the minutiae took the most time.

Another risk of writing this column was implying that all ageing doctors were impaired. Having had older doctors as wonderful mentors, I wanted to acknowledge their laudable contributions to medicine.

Due to constantly looming deadlines, I tend not to ask other people for rapid feedback, but this time, a friend provided valuable insights to strengthen my column. He suggested the idea that institutions could help ageing doctors by providing flexibility and transitional roles. He also proposed seeking real-world feedback on doctors from a cross-section of their coworkers and, potentially, patients, which I found intriguing.

I wanted to uphold the honour of the medical profession by highlighting how seriously doctors took their duty of care. This helped me state that one of my cognitively impaired colleagues thought he did too – but he lacked insight into his condition. This observation wrapped my reasons for the importance of an objective assessment of a doctor's capacity.

Finally, to really involve readers, I included the link for public submissions and emailed the Medical Board to expect feedback after the closing date.

The column generated enthusiastic debate and was the top

From Thinking Clearly to Writing Clearly

trending column across the *Guardian* opinion section. Amidst my correspondents was a litigation lawyer who wrote that he very much looked forward to and enjoyed the clarity of thought I brought to a range of medical issues. I felt proud of this comment because the hardest part of writing a column is being clear in one's own mind about what matters.

7

Simplifying Complex Topics

> 'The trouble with too many words
> is that they hide thoughts.'
> Benjamin Franklin

I love to write but finding what to write about every fortnight is something I could delegate.

In the weeks I am especially busy seeing patients, I am tempted to take the easy way and write about a familiar subject. With increasing years of work and life, such topics have grown. They include cancer, end-of-life care, medical ethics, and doctor–patient communication. Others involve aged care, migrant health, judicious utilisation of healthcare services and futile medicine. From a large library of experiences, it is not too difficult to pick out useful ones and find a message for public interest.

But I also need to guard against repetition, for my own sake and for the sake of my readers. And I do relish a challenge.

Doctors envision their work in terms of scope of practice. Many prefer to perform at the comfortable end, repeating familiar conversations and procedures over decades. They help patients by reliably delivering a service they are practised at and there is a lot to be said for steadfastness of thought and process. Then there are doctors who strive to practise at the top of their scope. They seek new ways of communicating, treating, operating and thinking and seldom sit still professionally. This is how healthcare improves for the average consumer.

When I reflect on caring for my gravely ill patients, obviously expert knowledge matters greatly, but in a high-quality healthcare system this is expected. So, empathy and compassion are foremost in my mind. Appearing erudite or being across the latest data often matters less to patients than walking with them through hardship.

In these instances, one doesn't have to look hard for proof of benefit because it shows up in the way of a grateful note, flowers, brownies baked with love or even an invitation to a funeral. I have learnt that there are some comfortable, predictable ways of practising medicine that can also help patients.

Writing is different. Here, I never truly belong in a comfort zone. Writing regularly challenges me to pursue hard goals that demand sweat and effort. The gratification of the process of becoming a better writer keeps me striving. I enjoy writing but it still doesn't feel as second nature as the practice of medicine. Perhaps it never will.

Starting with a sense of impossibility

The columns I most enjoy creating and writing are those where I start with a faint sense of impossibility. The topic is too big, too complicated, politically charged, socially awkward, or any number of things to wrestle into a 900-word column.

At these moments, a voice inside me says, 'I don't think I can do that' and another one says, 'But wouldn't it be great if it worked?' For me, the joy of writing is in entertaining that second voice.

Here is an instance of simplifying complex topics for the public.

In January 2025, the US Surgeon General, Vivek Murthy, issued a report linking alcohol with cancer that made global headlines. Alcohol is ingrained in the culture of many parts of the world, including Australia.

The ill effects and dangers of alcohol are well known but media commentary usually focuses on complications like road trauma, violence, workplace absenteeism and the high social cost of drinking.

The Surgeon General's report zoomed in on cancer risk, outlining the various cancer diagnoses caused by alcohol, either via direct contact with body tissue or through metabolites and hormonal fluctuations. In essence, drinking excessively raises the lifetime risk of cancer by about five per cent. Most people are unaware of this.

When this report came out, it was the peak of summer in Australia and people were still engaged in post-Christmas festivities. Australians are some of the heaviest and most regular drinkers in the world, so unquestionably, this was a matter of public interest.

But the world spends nearly two trillion US dollars on alcohol, many people like to drink responsibly and enjoy it, and the notion of an opinion piece meddling with this affinity frankly made me a little cold. But once the idea was in my head, overlooking it seemed like passing on a challenge. As I have said elsewhere, periodically tackling difficult things is a road to satisfaction and improvement. So, about to take a one-week holiday (during which my first column of the year was due), I decided to write about the perennially controversial issue of how much alcohol is enough.

Most people are either unaware of or ignore consumption

guidelines, which are admittedly confusing. My first thesis was 'There is no safe level of drinking'. This advice is backed by the World Health Organization and some countries, but as I tossed it around in my head, I thought that this was not the place for a strident tone.

I revised my thesis to, 'Here is what you should know about alcohol to make up your own mind'. This aligned with my own philosophy of equipping people with information to help them decide.

To break the column into manageable chunks, I chose three main points. One, Australian drinking statistics and why they matter. Two, the bottom line of the Surgeon General's report and how other countries warn their citizens. And then, as I wrote, I recalled all the people who said they drank for heart health, an example of an anticipated argument that needed addressing.

For each of the main points, I located at least one credible link that was not behind a paywall, easy to do with the amount of free information on the internet.

I used the opening anecdote as a touchpoint to connect with readers about a sensitive issue. And I spent the most time crafting the concluding lines. As someone who doesn't drink, it would have been easy to take a strong stance against the habit. But it only takes a moment to realise that in life, we take daily risks, from walking and driving to eating and exercising, so it was especially important to avoid being puritanical. Thinking about the various messages during the Covid pandemic that backfired made me add in the line about exaggeration being the enemy of credibility, true for work and home. (How many times do we ask our children to get off the screen because 'it's terrible for you'?)

I mentioned that I was on holiday with my children when this column was due, so a word on how I finished my task. My idea to write on the flight proved unrealistic as I fell asleep. The next day, when we were out exploring a new city, a loose construct formed in my mind. The following day, when the teenagers were still asleep, I woke up to write most of the body, got stuck at the conclusion and left it for another time.

Later that evening, I sat down to write a conclusion, keen to temper my tone and provide sensible advice. By the time I was satisfied, I had catapulted over 1,000 words.

Nonetheless, I believe that a longer article is easier to edit than a blank page. I trimmed the anecdote without losing the intent and, once I was close to 900 words, proofread my column and filed it.

A quick email exchange with the editor about one or two clarifications followed and the column was ready for publication well in advance. One compliment I like hearing from my editors is that I always file punctually, which means they can get organised without having to pester me. I consider this to be a minimum requirement of professionalism.

Once I had sent it, it was blissful to not think at all about writing for the last few days of my holiday. Given people's penchant for alcohol, I was curious to see how the column would be received, noting that the headline (which I don't write) was quite benign. ('The links between alcohol and cancer are clear, but most Australians are unaware of the risks.')

It was one of the most read columns of the day and generated expected discussion. A doctor (who had written a column in a medical publication proposing extending Dry January to the rest of the year) told me that some of her friends had told her to 'go away'. This made me especially glad to have moderated my approach.

Another example of the importance of simplicity

Continuing with the theme of simplifying complex topics, here is another example.

Hearing impairment is one of the most common avoidable causes of cognitive impairment. As society ages, millions more will need assistance to maintain good hearing and social connections. This abstract idea struck a personal chord when my mother's mild hearing impairment worsened after an infection and, like many elderly people, she was scammed by a hearing aid commercial in a shopping mall.

The Australian government provides subsidies for eligible patients to acquire hearing aids. However, few people appreciate that the subsidy system offers a choice: patients can either receive a fully subsidised device or use the subsidy towards a more expensive device for their specific needs. They are also unaware that the subsidy is only available once every five years, limiting how often people can replace inappropriate devices. Consumers and professionals have long complained that the system is flawed and outdated, but it was only after my mother was affected that I had cause to find an excellent independent report about an industry plagued with problems. Had I read it earlier, I could have been a much stronger advocate for my mother; now I felt responsible for assisting other people like her.

Faced with the challenge of condensing a dense report into a 900-word advocacy column, my first instinct was to pass. But my desire to democratise information and penchant for a challenge sent me back to create a shortlist of questions and ask an audiologist friend to explain an area I had zero practical knowledge of.

In writing this column, I began with a simple question: what three things about hearing aids do I want an informed consumer to know?

As I have mentioned previously, covering too many points risks diluting the message. Clear thinking leads to clear writing, so I picked the following questions.

- **Eligibility:** Who qualified for the government subsidy and how could one access it?
- **Subsidy:** How did it work and what were the limitations?
- **Scams:** What did they look like and how to avoid them?

Writing down these points made it possible for me to segment the writing process.

Starting the column with my mother's lived experience with her consent made the column relatable. Ending it with a call to action felt appropriate.

It can be tricky writing on topics not within one's remit, so I was relieved when expert audiologists supported my stance and thanked me for shedding light on a sensitive issue in their circles. This column was shared widely and was a springboard for a submission to government. Many readers were grateful for the plain-language advice, some saving or forwarding it for future reference.

Writing simply is not simple

Academic articles often involve intricate details and technical jargon. In 2024, the *Economist* newspaper tracked 347,000 English-language PhD abstracts awarded by British universities and published over 200 years. The dataset was produced by the British Library. The Flesch reading-ease test measures readability, where a score of 100 indicates writing that can be understood by a fourth-grade student (aged about ten). A score lower than 30 is considered very difficult to read. A *New York Times* article scores around 50 and a *CNN* article around 70. The *Economist* found that in every discipline, from natural sciences to the humanities and social sciences, readability has fallen. In the latter two fields, the average Flesch score has dropped from 37 in the 1940s to just 18 in the 2020s.

With the demise of clear writing, it is even more important and exciting to distil important messages and connect with the public.

Simplifying complex topics is time consuming. For the column listed below, I spent an estimated eight hours over two days just reading and digesting the report and thinking about how to structure my column. But I thought that if my advocacy empowered even a fraction of readers, it would be worthwhile. As an aside, versatile writing helps keep you engaged and avoid the risk of becoming predictable.

Time permitting, it can be helpful to ask a non-expert if your thoughts are cogent and expressed as clear writing. After all, writing for the public is catering to non-experts. Whenever I write about things I don't know, I admit it unabashedly and, in the process, gain valuable and enthusiastic help. I am constantly struck by how much people like being asked their advice.

Simple but powerful writing demands patience and iteration. But while the initial process can seem daunting, it is this very challenge that makes writing such a fulfilling endeavour and creates good writers.

TIPS

1. Embrace the challenge of simplifying complex topics.
2. Edit yourself ruthlessly, or someone else will.
3. Write to be understood by a non-expert.

Simplifying Complex Topics

Why Australia must break the conspiracy of silence and restore hearing to the most vulnerable

It is time the government listened to the experts and reined in misleading providers

5 July 2023

Guardian

'If I don't do something about my hearing, I fear I could lose my mind.'

While hearing loss is indeed a strongly modifiable risk factor for dementia, it shouldn't have taken this pronouncement for me to pay attention.

For some years, my mother has observed that her hearing isn't as good as it used to be, which describes nearly three-quarters of people like her over age 70. But she seemed to get by in social settings and sometimes at home we just shouted a little louder.

Attracted by an ad for free hearing aids at a mall, she met an obliging man who, after perfunctory testing, declared that she needed hearing aids. She demurred due to the stigma but the man kept calling and texting every week. Eventually, the combination of 'wasting the poor man's time' and her own concern led her back to the shop, where she was fitted with a pair of hearing aids. To her mind, their being 'free' reasonably mitigated any downside. 'If they work, that's good; if not, they are free.'

For my part, I was glad that, not being a native English speaker, she had managed to navigate an aspect of her health by herself, something I have long advocated for.

Following a mild bout of Covid, her hearing worsened. Decongestants, medications and doctor visits followed, all in vain.

Amid exuberant conversation, she would ask quizzically: 'Did I miss something?' She started keeping quiet, pretending to be happy just being among us. But it was when she stopped answering her doorbell that my alarm bell rang.

I checked if she was wearing her hearing aids – the best devices won't work from the inside of a drawer. But diligence got her nowhere, so she trekked back to the provider, who changed the batteries without explaining if that was the problem. It was not. Disheartened, she went to a second provider, who tested her hearing ('for free') and told her what she already knew – that she had poor hearing.

He lobbed her to the first provider who said that because she had sought a second opinion, she was no longer eligible to receive his services and should come back after five years to receive another 'free' product.

Watching this complete disempowerment from the sidelines finally got to me. What kind of providers were these? And what would five years of hearing impairment do to her quality of life?

My grand ambition that my mother be her own advocate had stalled – it was time for me to step in.

But where to begin?

My knowledge of the ear stops at the (Latin) names of the three bones of the middle ear. I last interpreted an audiometry graph as a medical student. Most of my patients have hearing aids that they either don't wear or turn off to spare me the ringing sounds that drive them mad. In search of answers, I turned to Google and luckily landed on an independent expert report. I read it in one sitting, all 200 pages, my eyes widening at every finding.

The Australian government funds the Hearing Services

Program to a tune of more than $531m but, established in 1997, it still has no statement of purpose or specific objectives.

Various cohorts are eligible for assessment and, if appropriate, partially or fully subsidised hearing devices. In 2019–20, an estimated 4 million people experienced hearing loss, 2 million met the eligibility criteria but only 39% of eligible people participated. The usual demographics missed out – the Indigenous, aged care residents, culturally and linguistically diverse and rural dwellers.

The whole report is excellent but I was drawn to the section on consumer choice.

While the program aspires to 'consumer sovereignty', consumers have little idea of the high stakes involved in choosing an initial provider, which affects what services they are offered. Vertical integration is commonplace, where the manufacturer or distributor controls the clinic and fails to disclose sales incentives. Seven out of ten providers supply over 90% of devices to their clients from only one manufacturer.

The government fully subsidises 200 hearing devices and partially subsidises tenfold more. Patients can accept a fully subsidised model or use the government subsidy to purchase a partially subsidised model; the out-of-pocket cost ranges between $150 and $15,000.

Despite a duty to disclose price, subsidy, incentives, product features, maintenance, repairs and replacement, compliance is patchy and formal accountability poor.

In the worst of both worlds, choice is constrained, and the consumer is unaware.

The expert report seems prescient in identifying every problem my mother encountered.

Knowing what I do now, what would I have done differently?

First, I would have paid better attention to my mother's milder problem because arresting hearing loss at an early stage affects quality of life, mood and cognition.

Even a cursory search for government services would have led me to the Hearing Services Program website and given me a roadmap. And had I read the independent expert report freely available on the internet, I would have been a more confident consumer, aware that the Australian Competition and Consumer Commission had repeatedly cautioned unethical providers.

And, much as I hate to admit it, I would have assumed that an elderly woman who is not fluent in English, can't hear well, is emotionally upset and trusts every provider to do the right thing had an early disadvantage.

After learning the difference between an audiometrist and a clinical audiologist, I switched to the latter.

She wasn't 'free' and neither were the hearing aids now that the one-time government subsidy had been squandered on a useless product. But she was a consummate professional who dwelled on every aspect of communication, tested hearing via more than one method, provided comprehensive information, and encouraged my parents to take their time making an expensive purchase. You know exceptional service when you see it.

As a public hospital doctor, I find few things more upsetting than the waste of taxpayer funds, this time by my own family who didn't know better. But with one in four Australians predicted to experience hearing loss by 2050, we won't be the last ones in this predicament.

To hear properly is to be connected to the world. It is time the government listened to the experts, reined in misleading providers, and put our money in our ears.

About this column

In writing this column, I took a risk.

I knew nothing about the industry beyond my mother's bad experience. But once I read the report and decided to write about the issue, I enjoyed the intellectual challenge.

It was a relief to note audiologists recommend every word as being true. Another reader wrote about noticing the problem but finally understanding why so many people complained about their hearing aids. And there was a touching note from someone whose parents were involved in the early advocacy and education movement to help the hearing impaired.

As a bonus, this column was featured in the *Guardian*'s 'Top 5 reads', which amplified (no pun intended) its impact.

8

Developing your Writing Career

'First I did it to please myself, then I did it to please
my friends, and finally I did it for money.'
Ferenc Molnár

The Hungarian playwright Ferenc Molnár is credited with originally comparing the progression of his writing career to prostitution. His matter-of-fact observation gives me cause to wince and smile.

In 2012, the editor of a glossy magazine called me out of the blue and asked if I had thought about being a regular columnist. I thought it was a prank, but he offered an endearing confession: he had not read my book but his wife, dealing with a parent's terminal illness, had been moved by *Tell Me the Truth*, my early-career memoir of being an oncologist. That book had been a surprise finalist for an Australian literary award (won by a former prime minister), and when she suggested he hire me to write a regular column, he trusted her judgement.

I remember exactly where I was when he called: on the trampoline with three little children, the youngest still on my hip. My immediate reaction was a thrill quickly clouded by doubt.

I wondered how on earth I would manage part-time work, full-time parenting and a 'proper' writing job. But even as I feared compromising my reputation with subpar writing, every fibre of my being itched to say yes to this exciting and serendipitous opportunity.

I climbed off the trampoline, set my child down, and paced around the house as I listened to the editor's proposal. Instead of agreeing to write for one year, I insisted on a trial period of a few months. It seemed to me a dignified escape clause in case I wasn't good enough. I was a long way from having confidence in my own work.

I was also apprehensive about what the publicity of being a columnist would mean for my career. Medicine was more than a job; it was my vocation – and I needed the healthcare system and its people on my side. The editor must have encountered a few nervous writers in his time given the forbearance with which he treated my caveats. On a practical note, he advised me to write as a private citizen without mentioning an institutional affiliation. As a journalist, he was well versed in the layers of bureaucracy and his advice would prove astute.

I felt so indebted to the publication that the idea of getting paid for my privilege never crossed my mind. The editor mentioned a figure, and I said yes, lacking the confidence to believe that I could make an income from writing. Much later, I realised how generous and upright he had been in guarding my interests when I was naïve, gratitude I have subsequently expressed in person.

After the phone call ended and the editor cheerily told me how glad he was to have me on board, I wiped my eyes and let the news sink in. I bet he had no idea of the significance of the moment.

It's instructive that despite my burning desire to write, my first response to a real opportunity was, 'I don't know if I can.' I suspect this may be especially familiar to professional women. I have subsequently spent my career resisting, and helping other women resist, that feeling.

Shortly afterwards, a photographer arrived at my house and shot a hundred photos to yield one for my first work inside the glossy magazine, whose cover proudly announced, 'our new health columnist'.

Louis Pasteur (of pasteurisation fame) observed that fortune favoured the prepared mind. It had taken me years of unknowing preparation to get to this point. I had written a journal since age ten and submitted essays and poems to writing competitions, medical journals and various newspapers for years. All the while, I had longed to be a regular writer, never thinking it would happen to me. I had no connections.

When the opportunity came, I want to say it was a dream come true but frankly, I didn't even know to dream that dream. I neither knew any columnists who wrote for the public nor any doctors who did so. It's hard to be what you can't see.

Discovering the practicalities of writing

The first thing I discovered was how much I loved the whole act of writing for the public. I became more observant of current events, my own work and what was in the public interest – and how my writing might illuminate issues or advocate for change.

I was allowed to write a maximum of 1,000 words. It was hard work: no room for empty words, tautness in every line. Sometimes, a seemingly good idea or even an entire column was discarded by me or, occasionally, an editor.

I quickly learnt a few things: in a busy phase of life, I never had an uninterrupted block of time to write a draft column from beginning to end; my work was necessarily piecemeal. This forced me to write short segments, but write them well so they might require minimal editing.

I also learnt to write wherever I could: perched on the edge of the bathtub; at the kitchen table; the sidelines of the soccer pitch; and waiting for all manner of kids' activities and appointments. I love the feel of writing with a nice pen on good-quality paper, but I invested in a light laptop whose best feature was that it started up instantly.

I can happily verify my own advice to you, dear reader: it is possible to write little by little.

I also discovered the opportunity cost of writing, which economists define as the loss of alternatives when one makes a choice. I was publishing only one column a month, but with young children, just this one addition stretched me. This made me loath to increase my hours at the hospital, which made me anxious about my career and how my professionalism might be judged by others.

Finally, I had to learn to manage my guilt that as a mother of young children (three under age five), I was being selfish. I had a strong and proud family behind me, so the guilt, while my own concoction, was undeniably there. Writing did not help my kids and, in fact, made me distractible and took me away from them. The notion that a happy mother made for happy children felt true on paper but abstract in real life. Like all mothers, I made many adjustments while deciding to hang on to writing as long as I could. It would be years before my children would (rarely) read me and (sometimes) express pride in my work. Today, they are all teenagers, increasingly busy with their own lives and sometime beneficiaries of a writer mother.

I can only now say categorically that we are all happy that I continued to write.

My two years of writing for the glossy magazine were wonderful. I loved the whole process: envisioning a topic; discussing it with my editors; the ensuing wordplay; then the edits and, finally, publication day. I loved buying the newspaper, finding the glossy magazine, seeing the title of my column featured on the front cover and looking inside for the first time. Soon, the emails and handwritten letters from readers would start arriving. They would share observations, stories and suggest ideas for future columns.

When the publisher suddenly announced that the magazine was no longer profitable and was folding, I was hit by a feeling akin to grief. I remember that phone call, too, although not as clearly as the one offering me a job. In an inauspicious ending, my final column mourning the loss of the magazine was rejected and I was told to rewrite it.

So glaring was the hole in my regular writing life that for months I used any time between patient care to contact every publication I could think of. While I now had some name recognition and most editors were polite, hiring me as a columnist was not on anyone's wish list.

Disheartened, I kept writing in my journals but found myself longing for an assignment and a deadline. As many creative people attest, a fallow mind turned out to be just the prescription for the rich yield of my next book. Spurred on by a moving patient experience, I wrote my second book. At less than 100 pages, *Dying for a Chat: The Breakdown of Doctor–Patient Communication* emphasised the importance of advance care directives to help people at the end of life. I had written this book because I needed distraction and was astonished when it won an award that I didn't even know my publisher had entered it for. I was grateful for the recognition but my best reward was the boost to my flagging confidence in the idea of writing for the public, although I would be biding my time for some more years.

Pitching your writing ideas

I was attending an international conference in Chicago in 2013 when I saw the news that the *Guardian* newspaper had opened an Australian office. Taking a punt, I wrote to the editor, Katharine Viner, proposing an occasional column on medicine and humanity. Busy embedding the paper, she nonetheless responded warmly, if only to say that, as a former science reporter, she liked the idea, but it was not an immediate priority. Out of options, I decided to see it as a positive that she wasn't saying 'never', only 'not now'.

Buoyed by this response, I kept asking her periodically, enough to appear interested but not too frequently to be pesky. Unbelievably, she took a chance on me and my first column for the *Guardian* appeared in 2013. I remember the morning it was published I was seeing patients. I printed out the column and excitedly thrust it into the hands of my nonplussed colleagues. (It would be an early introduction to the reality that no one is more thrilled by your writing than you.)

My first *Guardian* column addressed a new Australian study of doctors' mental health. I had picked this topic carefully, using some of the tips I have talked about. It was making news; I had an insider's view, and the matter was in the public interest. My main point was that doctors who are themselves unwell can't make their patients well.

But if I had hoped that writing one column would be an automatic in, I was slated for more disappointment. My column fared well but soon, I was back to pitching and suffering silence and many rejections interspersed with a few nods.

Looking back, something I did well was not take the rejections personally but as a symptom of a busy news cycle. I kept thinking of new ideas and let the editors' disinterest glide over me, committing myself to patient care and submitting occasional essays to the *New England Journal of Medicine* to keep up my writing habit. Being published in the *Journal* always made me happy because it was a competitive field and, with every hard-won publication, I grew as a writer.

Just before Christmas in 2013 I received an unexpected phone call from the *Guardian*. Apparently, the handful of ad hoc columns I had written had attracted enough reader attention that the newspaper wanted to make room for me as a regular columnist. I remember being in the playground of my children's primary school, surprised, thrilled and, again, self-doubting all at once.

The editor asked me how often I wanted to write. It was like asking my dog how often he wanted to walk – always.

This time, I backed myself. Writing monthly for the glossy magazine had seemed too little but a weekly column would stretch me. Every two weeks might be the Goldilocks interval. The editor cheerfully agreed and, after telling me to send a headshot photo, hung up, leaving me to collect my thoughts before collecting my oldest child from primary school. I stifled my doubts about how I would write with two children still at home.

Along with the day I was admitted to medical school and my first day as an intern, the day I became a *Guardian* columnist, was decidedly a high point of my life. Of course, there are many memorable personal moments, but in terms of career, I was now a doctor and a 'real' writer.

I was so elated that I could not even think about the opportunity cost of filing a column every two weeks. Somehow, I would have to do it.

Eventually, I learnt that I would be paid less than at the glossy magazine. Even though I had no bargaining power I knew that I was being handed a significant opportunity to shape public discourse. I traded payment for a public platform – acutely conscious and very grateful that my day job gave me a freedom not available to many writers.

Payment for your writing

Good writing entertains and engages but nearly always doesn't pay well. I remember sitting next to a heralded children's author who had just won another prize. She told me that it was the first year she was able to pay the bills on her own. Moderating my expectations about the proceeds of writing has been useful in limiting resentment and enjoying the journey.

It is possible that the many hours I spend on writing could be more generously paid elsewhere but for me, that would missing the point. My writing helps me weather life's storms and make sense of my world. I am now at a stage of life where I see routine, exhaustion and burnout creeping into the lives of many of my mid-to-late-career colleagues. But an unexpected benefit of writing for the public has been a regular calibration of my mental health. In an emotionally demanding job like oncology, not having a 'release valve' is a recipe for stress, but a parallel career in writing has accorded me balance and, I hope, longevity.

A focus on quality writing has slowly anchored other interesting opportunities. There has been an organic growth of speaking invitations, keynote addresses and advisory board positions. When my columns are reproduced for teaching and training, I am invited to discuss them with students.

Lately, I have been teaching online writing courses at my alma maters, Harvard and the University of Chicago.

Enthusiasm for writing is infectious. Talking about writing inspires me to write and I love helping others realise their aim of publication. They remind me of my old self – and it's wonderful to pay it forward.

Altogether, these occasions beyond direct patient care open interesting avenues of conversation with people I wouldn't otherwise have met, another way of staying engaged with the world.

A final word on pay. I must have read countless advice columns on knowing one's worth and seeking fair pay, an issue especially germane to women. It took me a decade to ask for a pay rise.

I was prompted to do this after noticing that my columns are well read and prompt animated discussion. I am punctual, don't attract complaints and write with integrity. I had trouble taking the advice that I have given to other writers but finally, I worked up the courage and, to my surprise, the *Guardian* responded positively.

Here are some things you ought to keep in mind about developing a writing career.

Good writing deserves fair compensation. Most publications

pay a nominal amount and it's for you to decide if this meets your expectations. Naturally, it's okay to be an occasional writer, for instance when something catches your eye, especially if this provides a balance between making an income and using your creativity.

In my earliest days of writing, when I was either meagrely paid or not paid, I was happy to receive a free education in pitching, writing, publishing and navigating the aftermath. This helped me mature and build a public profile. I can see why this may not be sustainable for others.

Column-writing has improved my thinking and writing skills and fostered the discipline of writing books, which is a labour of love. This book that you are reading has been in the making for more than two years and has gone through so many iterations that there are days I can't bear to look at the manuscript again. This is quite normal, by the way.

When it comes to columns, I can now write faster with fewer drafts. The seven books I have written so far generate a modest income but, more important to me, are readily available to the public through local libraries, the National Library of Australia and the US Library of Congress. To me, this feels like a meaningful contribution to society.

After the initial pitch for my book, *A Better Death*, was rejected (for being 'immature'), I felt a familiar pinch of despondency. I thought this was the end of my book-writing career. But as is often the case, rejection can also refuel ambition.

In between moping and dreaming, I wrote a book for high school students called *What It Takes to Be a Doctor*, based on the advice I routinely give to aspiring doctors. My publisher paid no advance but agreed to publish a kind of book that is not its mainstay. Today, it is stocked by school libraries and used by guidance counsellors, parents and students. I sign many copies as gifts.

It is satisfying to know that the book helps people become better informed about a career in medicine, which is good for future patients.

Writing can lead to opportunities

In 2025, the National Library of Australia invited me to contribute to an oral history and a collection of my writings to highlight the importance of humanity in medicine. If the exhibit inspires change in some aspect of healthcare, it will be a just reward. My inclusion has also prompted me to think of other writers whom I could share the platform with. I could not have foreseen any of these interesting developments when I first began writing.

If you are a writer with an academic connection, consider writing for a platform such as *The Conversation*. By uniting scholars with journalists, this site educates and informs the public while editors help hone your writing skills. Contributions are unpaid but they increase exposure and experience in public communications. I sometimes link to this site in my columns. These days, well-written pieces on various online sites can be amplified via social media and generate fresh opportunities for writing.

Unexpectedly, my writing has helped with board appointments. I especially like being on one board that does not remunerate its advisers but donates to a charity of their choice. Every year I look forward to deciding how to disburse my funds. In the last few years, I have supported the building of a literacy program at a primary school almost exclusively attended by migrant and refugee children and established a science scholarship for high school students. I also support the work of the Asylum Seeker Resource Centre, an organisation I volunteered with when I was a trainee doctor and whose founder became my close friend. This has been my small patch of experimenting in effective altruism.

In concluding, I want to acknowledge again that a creative career may be unsuitable for people who need to earn an income.

Talent should be adequately recognised and remunerated. Ultimately, we must be selective about how to balance our time when following creative pursuits.

But I also hope to have shown you that when writing for the public, the sheer civic engagement and opportunity for growth has much to recommend it.

TIPS

1. Writing for money takes persistence and adaptability.
2. If possible, don't always write for the money, but do consider the opportunity cost.
3. Quality writing can open other avenues of income and interest.

Doctors are more likely to be depressed? I'm not surprised

A new survey found that one in ten doctors entertained suicidal thoughts in the past year. Those are sobering numbers illustrating a problem I'm all too familiar with

9 Oct 2013

Guardian

I recently invited two friends, a neurosurgeon and an anaesthetist, to dinner. My husband is a GP and I am an oncologist – due to our schedules, it took us weeks to find a convenient date. Our friends arrived many hours late. The surgeon had been operating on a brand-new mum whose headaches revealed a brain tumour. He inserted a life-saving shunt that night, but her prognosis was grim. The anaesthetist had been monitoring another precarious situation where the patient's life still hung in balance. Earlier that day, my husband's elderly patient had suffered a near cardiac arrest while chatting to him. The waiting room was evacuated and sirens rang out. That same evening, I had received a tearful call from a terminally ill patient. He was in excruciating pain, the hospice was full, there was a long wait in emergency and he was frightened of dying. Could I help?

These were the accounts of our day as we greeted each other. Then the oven beeped, reminding us of a dinner many times reheated. In the course of just one day, we had been witness to serious and tragic life events; yet, as if observing a silent code of conduct, we never once mentioned those misfortunes as we ate. One such event once in a life might have ruined most people's appetite for food and company, but not ours. We were different.

That night, I didn't sleep. My thoughts turned to the young mother who would not see her baby grow up. And I fretted over my sick patient. I suspect we all had a disturbed night, our equanimity fractured by the fate of our patients. But I also knew that the next morning we would return to work, our facade repaired. For in that small space between sleep and wake, we would have consoled ourselves that bad things happen and our job as doctors is to not let ourselves feel too bad about them lest we fail our future patients.

A doctor's best debriefing tool after a hard day therefore turns out to be wilful forgetfulness. If you can minimise or, better still, normalise catastrophe, you can keep going. Except, as a recent Australian survey of more than 14,000 doctors and medical students shows, this attitude comes at a great cost. One in 10 doctors entertained suicidal thoughts in the past year, compared to one in 45 in the community. More than a quarter of doctors are highly likely to suffer from mental illness. Oncologists like me, who routinely deal with death, face an especially high risk, as do young women and international doctors. This laudable study has caused a collective gasp in the community but for most doctors, it has simply put sobering numbers to a problem we are all too familiar with. Far too many of us have lost a dear friend and able colleague to drugs, alcohol, crippling mental illness or suicide. Many more feel like helpless bystanders as we watch good doctors slowly self-destruct.

Every doctor knows that the very problems we counsel our patients for are those that beset us in far greater measure. So you might ask why intelligent, driven, capable doctors would ignore the warning signs that they know by rote. Again, the survey identifies what every doctor either knows or suspects: the stigma attached to mental illness is magnified within the medical profession. Doctors regard their mentally ill peers with uncertainty and fear. They consider them less capable and are less willing to hire them or work with them. It therefore makes sense to keep problems under wraps in an unsupportive environment.

For me, watching the journey of some of my mentally ill friends has been in turns frightening, unsettling and sad. It's a tightrope to envelop a colleague in understanding while protecting their patients from harm as a result of inattention. As a sympathetic observer, it is tempting to become impatient with at-risk doctors who don't or won't seek help, even though they have access to it. But it is also difficult to convince doctors to appreciate the extent of their problem, because we have been shaped to believe in our infallibility. Diseases afflict our patients; they don't touch us. Our patients are defined by their illness, while we are defined by our ability to cure their malady. Medical education shies away from discussing our vulnerabilities. Students and young doctors are rarely reminded that despite their hallowed place in society, they are prone to the same vicissitudes of life as everyone else. It is no wonder that when faced by personal catastrophe, a doctor's first response is to deny the problem exists.

Doctors have a long tradition of being considered different from the rest of society. But when it comes to mental illness, our serious differences are jeopardising our own health and that of our patients. The culture of medicine demands a change. To do any less would be to shortchange doctors and patients.

About this column

This was my very first column for the *Guardian*.

The content would be familiar to a healthcare professional but for a general audience, it was a window into the way doctors are trained and socialised. And since everyone sees a doctor at some point in their life, I thought it was important to discuss an issue that afflicts doctors at higher rates than many other professional workers.

The reception was mixed. Mental health professionals complimented it and added their own observations. Some readers thought this was another instance of highly paid doctors crying foul, others said that the column was short of solutions. They were right even though solutions to knotty problems are hard to pack into a tight column (thus underlining the importance of addressing a few points and doing it well). On reflection, I was new to a public role and would need more time and self-confidence to write with authority. I don't think it was my best column but how could it be when there was so much to learn about writing for a global audience?

Shakespeare called expectation the root of all heartache. But that day, I had no expectation of being a return writer let alone a regular columnist. If someone had told me that I'd still be writing for the *Guardian* more than ten years later, I wouldn't have believed it and, indeed, worried about what I'd possibly have to say.

That day, I allowed myself to feel the happiness of publishing at least one column in my life in a prominent newspaper. I printed out copies for my friends and my parents and even wrote a journal entry that began, 'Today, I published my first column in the *Guardian*.'

9

Writing for the Public

'What is written without effort is in general
read without pleasure.'
Samuel Johnson

The glossy magazine I wrote for, and enjoyed so much, cost money to buy and had a modest local distribution, so, while I poured myself into every column, I remained a relatively obscure writer. There were a few handwritten letters and, as my readership grew, many emails about people's experiences of the healthcare system. I appreciated and learned from every correspondent, but it wasn't until I was at the *Guardian* that I entered the public eye.

Apart from being two hundred years old and one of the world's most widely read English language newspapers, it carries the added appeal of not being behind a paywall. As I have written elsewhere, the words of its former editor, CP Scott, 'Comment is free, but facts are sacred', resonate with the doctor in me.

Writing for the *Guardian* has provided me with an unprecedented platform to express my views and explore ideas important to the public interest. It has also exposed me to more commentary and criticism. Therefore, navigating a public presence is an ongoing learning exercise.

Writing with a purpose

Good writing has the power to inform, inspire and advocate. Ill-considered writing has perhaps more power to diminish trust and sow discord. Modern writers are navigating a landscape marked by polarisation and instant confrontation. In today's digital age, where selective interpretations of tone and substance can fuel heated debate, it can be difficult to anticipate what will provoke whom. Complicating matters further is the lasting nature of our digital footprint where corrections and retractions can trigger a fresh round of commentary and scrutiny.

I am an insider in a healthcare system that matters to everyone because at some point, we will all need medical advice and assistance. I understand the complexities, nuances and failings of the system and am keen to democratise medicine. Perhaps this wish arises from having lived and volunteered in countries where the basic needs of patients have gone unmet through not being heard or resources being stretched.

But writing about a profession on which one also depends on for inclusion and income can be tricky, so people are curious what roadblocks a writer like me faces.

First, medicine contains heady successes but also a lot of failings, so it's not right to put a positive spin on everything.

Something that I believe has helped me gain the trust of readers is being honest about the good and bad; regarding myself as part of the problem *and* the solution; and avoiding armchair commentary.

I am quick to appreciate the healthcare system where I work, which is globally well regarded, and defend it against unfair perceptions. I am keen to elevate the good work of a wide range of health professionals, especially their research that typically gets buried in an academic journal behind a paywall. My colleagues tell me that they appreciate this contribution.

Judging by the worsening bureaucracy doctors face over routine patient care I cannot imagine receiving permission to write a column for the public unvetted by the hospital.

My editor and I emphasised the need to demonstrate my integrity through truthful, sensitive and balanced columns, for which I would carry responsibility. They were wise words, then and now.

Besides attracting an early irate email from public relations, I was thankfully left alone. Now, hospital libraries carry my books and use my columns for teaching. Thankfully, it is a sign of my writing adding value instead of causing concern.

Over the last decade, as the *Guardian* has found a foothold in Australia and retained a strong readership in other countries, I have found more global readers. This has made me even more conscious of honouring my professional obligations while continuing to write well. I am always finessing this fine balance.

I try to say less, listen more and be alert to people's sensitivities. I never set out to upset individuals, break confidences or unfairly blame institutions. I try to think of constructive suggestions while sharing personal regret where indicated. Most of all, I try to honestly interrogate ideas that matter to the public.

I tell the trainees I supervise that 'the system' is made up of each one of us; therefore, when we lament the system, it behoves us to look within. I hope that this inclusive approach to medicine has helped me co-opt rather than alienate readers.

It is estimated that for every doctor, there are up to eight administrators. I can imagine a risk-averse manager spooked by every imaginable downside of a doctor writing for the public. Therefore, it may have been prescient to have decided to seek forgiveness rather than ask permission.

Writing brings satisfaction

I love the immediacy of writing for the public and am always curious why readers react the way they do. I learn as much from the dialogue between readers as the remarks meant for me. Many readers are very well read and have access to information that is my gain.

Pointed or dismissive remarks from readers can pinch and it is irritating when well-intentioned writing is misinterpreted. Like every writer, I dislike it when my editors politely but firmly discard parts of my column, but overall, I look forward to the frisson of activity associated with the publication of a column. The night before my column is published, I go to bed with a sense of anticipation at having another chance at connecting with the world. Over time, my anxiety about how a column will be received has been replaced by a sense of wonder that I still get to write for the public.

Russell Lynes, the managing editor of *Harper's Magazine*, was right when he archly observed that no author dislikes being edited more than not being published.

Writing has also brought me a profound realisation: my public profile is important to me, but it really doesn't matter to anyone else. Each year I gain some more readers and followers on social media, but it hasn't changed the core of who I am.

My oldest friends are still my friends, my children still argue with me over chores and my proud parents might be convinced to read but one column a year. Much of my extended family has no idea that I write. My friends and family are just that and not my fans; our interactions comprise the usual mix of affections and tensions.

My colleagues take a passing interest in my writing. Writing well doesn't excuse me from fractious discussions around patient care.

Most movingly, I work in a disadvantaged area where many of my patients are not literate in any language. They judge me by the quality of my care, not the reach of my columns. In fact, only two people read every line of every column I write: me and my editor. This is the ultimate leveller.

Mark Twain said that a man cannot be comfortable without his own approval.

When writing, aim high but cultivate intrinsic satisfaction. The window dressings will come and go; take care to manage your inner writing life, the expectations and realities.

No one is more invested than me in the quality of my writing, so of course, no one is less forgiving. Remembering my speck-like presence in the vast world of publishing has been a most liberating realisation, in turn allowing me to write from a genuine place that makes writing joyful.

Key principles

Consider writing for the public and advocating for important issues as a useful contribution to society. Key principles you might benefit from include owning your work, avoiding unnecessary controversy, managing your relationship with social media and limiting a desire for external validation.

Owning your work is paramount. I once asked an editor out of curiosity what got a columnist fired. Without missing a beat, she said lying. Fabricating information is the fastest way of losing the trust of publishers and readers. Therefore, my foremost advice is to always tell the truth. When writing for the public, pay meticulous attention to the facts – they really are sacred. (Save the rest for your journal).

I never court controversy for its own sake, preferring to illuminate issues and engage readers with ideas that help them become more empowered healthcare consumers. I don't hector my readers. Making room in my own mind for different perspectives helps me temper my writing – just remembering this tip has helped me guard against sounding self-righteous and probably shielded my reputation.

Learning to navigate scrutiny and criticism is a vital aspect of writing for the public. We all want to be liked and affirmed. I love it when social media praises my work and readers send complimentary emails – I save each one and share some of the nicest ones with the editorial team so they too can bask in the praise. But compliments and criticism are bedfellows – to covet the compliments one must befriend the criticism. This can be bruising but also an undeniable opportunity for growth.

My social media presence is minimal. I read and reflect on online comments but rarely respond because I want to prioritise other commitments including patient care and raising my children.

While it feels impolite to not acknowledge the many wonderful comments, I channel the encouragement into better writing. And while I might privately rail against criticism, the same thinking applies. The one exception to this (outwardly) indifferent approach is if my writing genuinely hurts someone. Then, I am quick to act – more about this later.

Overall, I put the most effort into writing thoughtful pieces that speak for themselves and, once the column is published, quickly move on.

Writing for the public can be taxing in a lot of ways but it is also a lot of fun. Its lessons have helped me become more vulnerable, refine my communication and ultimately, become more confident using my moral compass to advocate for others.

TIPS

1. Writing for the public is a contribution to society.
2. To write without fear, cultivate inner satisfaction.
3. Treat your readers with courtesy and curiosity.
4. Criticism is an opportunity for growth.

Speaking Up – When Doctors Navigate Medical Hierarchy

24 January 2013

New England Journal of Medicine

He's the first patient of the day: admitted overnight, he's scheduled for surgery this morning. 'Do you want to catch him before or after?' the resident asks.

'Is there anything we need to do for him right away?' I say.

When she says that the night resident mentioned some pain issues, I decide to drop by.

As we walk, the resident describes the handover. The patient is a smoker in his early fifties who has a malignant pleural effusion that couldn't be managed at his local hospital. There was infection mixed with effusion, and antibiotics were ineffective. So he was referred here for video-assisted thoracoscopic surgery (VATS). After recovery, he would be transferred back closer to home for treatment of metastatic lung cancer.

In these situations, my role as a medical oncologist is usually limited to a courtesy call. It reassures the surgeon that there's an oncologist on board, and the patient appreciates seeing a friendly face without having to discuss serious news. But in the patient's room, what I find is unexpected. He's scrunched up in bed, tossing and turning, his sheets tangled between his legs. He's pale and uncomfortable, licking his lips, his IV fluids having run out. My immediate impression is that he's dying. But I remind myself that he's scheduled for surgery.

When I introduce myself, he's startled but speaks lucidly.

'I hear you are having an operation,' I say.

'Yes, they need to get this fluid off my chest.'

'Are you in pain?'

'Yes, it hurts like hell, doc. Every time I breathe, it stabs me.'

The resident hands me the sheet of inadequately charted pain relief. 'His kidneys are not great, so they've gone easy on the drugs,' she says.

'What's wrong with his kidneys?'

'He's been hypercalcemic for the last few days, though they gave him bisphosphonates.'

'You are going to have your chest drained soon,' I tell the patient, 'but let me arrange for you to get some pain relief right now. Also, you need some fluids to help your kidneys.'

'Thanks, doc,' the patient groans before resuming his fidgeting.

'You'll be OK,' I reassure him, but I'm unnerved: he looks delirious, and I have to check his chart to confirm that he's only 50. A nagging voice tells me he doesn't seem fit for surgery, but I suppress it, telling myself that a VATS is a straightforward palliative measure for patients drowning in an effusion. Outside the room, we run into the surgeon, whom I know well. He's about to meet the patient before the operation.

'We're done,' I say. 'By the way, he looks dry and needs better pain management, which I've attempted to fix.'

I pause, hoping for a sign of a reservation granting me permission to unleash my own mounting ones. But he simply says, 'I think the VATS will give the poor man relief. He's been struggling for days.'

We part ways, but when he's out of earshot, I tell my resident, 'I can't believe they operate on such patients; he just doesn't look right.'

'I suppose surgeons are used to it,' she shrugs, still convinced that we dabble in drugs whereas surgeons save lives. Seeking reassurance, I accept hers: if the surgeon admitted the patient, surely he can decide what's best. If necessary, the anaesthesiologist can call off the procedure. I quickly convince myself that I'm a bit player in this patient's journey. And that if my gut instinct says 'Don't operate', it's no stronger than the surgeon's instinct that says 'Get it over with'. The winning argument in my head is the one saying, 'Who are you to question a surgeon?' Although I know this attitude is baseless, it sits comfortably with me; my colleagues and I commonly defer to surgeons – considering them unequivocally right, unassailable or simply not worth antagonising. In an era when many patients have multiple reasonable treatment options, it seems more expedient to yield to the surgeon than go to bat for a patient. And that attitude is absorbed by generations of doctors who simply have to watch to learn.

In the clinic, I become enveloped in other patients' concerns. Later, when the resident tells me that the man made it through surgery, I'm relieved at not having embarrassed myself before the surgeon. I take the incident as a reminder to remain within the limits of my expertise. Of course the surgeon knew best. So the next day, when the resident points me toward the patient in the ICU, I'm stunned. 'Actually, he crashed and had to be intubated.'

The patient soon dies, as his stricken family looks on. Talking to his daughter, I'm taken aback by her understanding. 'Everyone was great – what else could we have asked for? Of course, we didn't expect this, but this is the way it is.'

The conversation leaves me disturbed. Is this really the best we could have done? I think not. For though we probably couldn't have changed the fact of his death, we held the circumstances in our hands. We could have cancelled the surgery, aggressively controlled his pain, and called an urgent family meeting to ascertain his wishes and be guided in shared decision making. But this model, to which we aspire, went astray, as it often does.

Days later, I speak to the surgeon. 'I feel so sorry that he died,' he reflects. 'I thought we could help him, but he was clearly too unwell to have an operation.'

The nagging voice returns to my head. Banking on our rapport, I say, 'I keep wishing that I had mentioned my doubts to you that morning. He looked like he was dying.'

Seizing on my comment, the surgeon asks, 'Why didn't you tell me?' He adds, with amazing honesty, 'When I walked out of his room, I wondered for a minute, but I told myself that since you had also seen him, he would be OK.'

'But that's exactly what I thought,' I protest. 'I thought you knew best and I shouldn't interfere.'

'If you had so much as mentioned your fears, I would have stopped,' he assures me remorsefully.

We realise that, each of us unsure, we gained confidence from the perceived assurance and expertise of the other. We unearth the other specialists who participated in the patient's care. The oncologist had wanted the infected effusion drained so he could safely commence chemotherapy. The respiratory physician had recommended referral to a larger centre for drainage. The infectious diseases physician had no more antibiotics to offer. The general internist bowed to the others, and the surgeon was approached as the next service provider in line. Tragically, no one person looked beyond the effusion to the whole patient.

Although he saw myriad specialists in his last week of life, he died lacking holistic care.

His obituary and a thank-you note reflect the grief of a family who lost their loved one more suddenly than anticipated. So, where does the buck stop? It seems unfair to pin it on the surgeon: he was merely the last clinician in line, no more morally responsible for the patient's death than any other participant in his care.

When I ask colleagues what they would have done, each recalls sometimes harbouring misgivings about another doctor's treatment of a patient but feeling unable or reluctant to comment, even when a patient's life might be threatened – preferring to swallow their discomfort rather than challenge another physician's viewpoint. Some are afraid, while others aim to 'live and let live', believing that there's no such thing as constructive criticism when it comes to one's peers. When a single perceived slight can spoil relationships that take years to create, doctors understandably tiptoe around each other.

Yet we all agree that if we were inadvertently harming our patient, we would appreciate being told.

Haunted by the incident and wishing never to repeat it, the surgeon and I agree on a simple pathway for decision making. He will question other hospitals more comprehensively before assuming that patients have been thoroughly worked up. In cases that aren't clear-cut, he will ask me to independently assess the patient's robustness for surgery. If uncertainty remains, we will jointly speak to the patient about our recommendations and record our conversation in the notes. One could argue that all these things happen with modern multidisciplinary team management, but not all team members eyeball the patient, and decisions are heavily influenced by the lead clinician.

Our agreement, forged from loss, has allowed some subsequent patients to avoid invasive, painful surgery in favour of better quality of life and others to undergo successful operations. The cooperation between internist and surgeon has been a salutary lesson for junior doctors who perceive the two as inimical. Early in training, we learn to spot the budding surgeon among internists, and it is worrisome that the main perceived point of differentiation is disparate notions of patient welfare. When internists jest about 'rescuing' surgical patients, they signal to surgeons that their role is to operate, while everyone else is the supporting cast. Apart from being disingenuous, this thinking engenders more stereotypical behaviours.

In a profession abounding with experts, no one person's expertise can always count for more. Although certain technical skills may be specialty-specific, there's a much broader range of skills on which no group has a monopoly. There's no chain of command in using gut instinct, showing concern for the whole patient, avoiding harm or curtailing futile care. We must recognise that debate is healthy and that, without open communication, we fill the space by guessing at each other's motives.

Recognising the pitfalls of blind adherence to hierarchy and broaching with a surgeon my misgivings about a patient: such an 'intervention' seems deceptively simple, uncontroversial, even cheap. Yet in my years of working with surgeons, it feels like the best thing we've done together for patients.

About this column

If I had known the reception it would elicit, I might have rethought the wisdom of writing this piece. If it had stayed within the *New England Journal*, it may not have caused a stir, but it just so happened that a doctor-writer for the *New York Times* read it, interviewed me and wrote a column about my column, as I now do when I read interesting pieces by other writers.

The *New York Times* coverage elicited a wave of scorn directed at me. Readers plied the comments section with criticism that I had not protected the patient from harm. Their words stung but were also a reminder that the reason I had written this essay was to reflect on having failed by my own standards.

The experience taught me one of the most important lessons of my career: when it came to safety, I never again failed to speak up for a patient.

10

Storytelling and Consent

> 'He who has a story to tell
> will always find listeners.'
> Ralph Waldo Emerson

I was recently invited to give a keynote talk at a medical conference, and I chose as my subject the story of being a physician-writer surrounded by compelling stories of the human condition. What better than to channel them into lessons for reflection, inspiration and advocacy? The talk was received warmly; people like stories.

While writing my speech, I had cast my mind back to when I was a young doctor finding my way. My early bosses disdained my lukewarm interest in what I found the sterile bits of academia. Obviously, I cared about the pathophysiology of disease and the search for effective cures starting at the research bench, but I also saw strong reason for the best technical care to coexist with an affinity for the human condition.

Surely, great science could go hand in hand with empathy for the many indignities of suffering. Why did this work have to be left to someone else?

On ward rounds and in clinics, I saw how the best doctors made patients feel seen, heard and understood, and how therapeutic the rapport was felt.

Conversely, I saw what happened when patients could not connect with their doctors. They avoided sharing important information and asking crucial questions. Some would later confide in nurses, but many never shared their stress and distress.

I remember thinking that being sick was challenging enough, so we should do everything humanly possible to improve the experience of illness. Thus, I was drawn to doctors who modelled the art of medicine without losing sight of its science.

Feeling alone in my thoughts, I began writing about some of my consequential experiences as a young doctor while longing to talk to like-minded people. It wasn't until I was a Fulbright scholar studying for a fellowship in medical ethics at the University of Chicago that I encountered doctors who were expert professionals *and* good storytellers.

What's more, no one who knew them thought that one skill somehow diminished the other. As I got to know them better, it dawned on me that I had been asking the right questions of the wrong people.

Finding mentors

One memorable mentor was a neonatal intensive care doctor, Bill Meadow, who led many of our ethics discussions. I loved the way he could slice through dense conversations to get to the point. Unsurprisingly then, he was also a clear writer who illuminated ethical dilemmas with his characteristic common sense. One day, when I self-consciously disclosed that I, too, aimed to be a writer someday, he replied emphatically, 'You *have* a book in you!'

Bill confidently introduced me to his writing friends as if I was the next big discovery. When my boss at the time, Mark Siegler, another prominent doctor and thinker about the art of medicine, found out, he invited me to a dinner where he sat me next to a famous author. The author and I struck up a warm association that continues to this day even after he went on to win major awards.

CS Lewis observed that the task of a teacher is not to cut down jungles but to irrigate deserts. My dad is a former university professor; in his commitment to uplifting students, I saw a living example of this observation.

Bill's confidence in me as a writer when I had none in myself changed my entire outlook. Earlier, I had felt pretentious for wanting a dual career as a doctor and writer. But Bill's one sentence of belief was the fuel that lit my fire. When I became a published writer, he was one of my greatest supporters who read every *Guardian* column and periodically sent a cheery message when he loved a piece. This continued until his untimely death. I still miss him.

Mark has retired but, after enabling my writing career, retains a touching interest in it. It felt like coming full circle when he asked me to contribute an essay about writing to an ethics journal that he guest-edited.

At my last visit, he and his wife presented me with a beautiful diary as a symbol of our long friendship.

The third person I met in my formative phase of writing is Lainie Ross, a paediatrician, ethicist and an exceptionally clear thinker (and thus, writer). As a mother to two girls, she was an early role model for me well before I had children. Watching her pursue a passion for medicine, advocate for her disadvantaged patients, always have a paper or textbook in the making, and be an involved mother helped me deal with my hesitation about heading towards an unconventional career.

The people who gave me a head start were joined by many others along the way in helping me believe that I could do well at more than one thing. I note their impact on my life to underline the importance of finding open-minded people who will help you rise in new ways.

Telling a story

The writer Miguel de Cervantes called the pen the tongue of the mind. What I most look forward to in writing is the chance to marshal my thoughts into a narrative.

Stories have a unique power to convey a message and connect with readers. In my work, I bear daily witness to difficult, remarkable and inspiring situations which are food for thought. Stories invite my readers to empathise, connect, and sometimes, benefit from what I have learnt.

Medicine is a profoundly human pursuit, so it's no surprise that my patients lie at the heart of my stories. For instance, when we encounter phrases like 'long waitlists', 'near-miss events', 'communication gaps' or 'medical miracles' in the news, we may gloss over them unless we are personally affected. However, in describing the waitlisted patient in constant pain due to a debilitatingly arthritic hip, the woman who narrowly escaped death from unrecognised sepsis, or the child saved by a life-changing liver transplant, abstract concepts come to life.

Recently I saw on the news that a toddler had died after an accident at a notoriously dangerous intersection near my hospital.

On one hand, the tragedy was indistinguishable from many other road traumas, but I noted the family were new refugees and remembered how my refugee patients recall the myriad ways they are tested by life in a new country.

One is road rules when their home country had neither rules nor roads. In my mind, the tragedy was of course the toddler who died, but the object lesson could be preventing such deaths through education. A column for the public, then, could advocate for community resources and common goodwill to help refugees in our community assimilate in simple ways.

You may have come across the striking six-word 'story' attributed to Ernest Hemingway.

'For sale: baby shoes, never worn.' Despite much being left to the imagination, those six words provoke curiosity, concern and perhaps pathos.

I often remind myself that if a sentiment can be conveyed in six words, my quota of 900 is practically opulent.

Privacy and consent

But of course, the stories I tell are not entirely mine. I write about my part in things that happen to other people, conscious and grateful that the moment I walk into work, I bump into stories. All writers can be accused of some form of appropriation. My job is a chance to serve patients and use my experiences to educate and empower others – and do so ethically.

When writing about my patients, I think of Graham Greene, who said that there is a splinter of ice in the heart of every writer. At some point, I make a calculation to take a deeply personal event to someone else and turn it into a column. The difficulty of translating sacrosanct stories into writing for the public is in navigating consent. Here is how I think about this important issue that, when handled well, can bring satisfaction and relief – and when not, can end in tears.

Many writers are rightly apprehensive about mentioning real people and situations due to the potential for backlash, embarrassment, or even legal consequences. In an era of permanent digital footprints, safeguarding other people's privacy is imperative. It's also essential to understand the nuances of consent and distinguish what was said on the record versus off the record.

I have always understood that seeking informed consent is my responsibility. An editor should never need to verify this, even though my editors occasionally do because they are doing their job well.

I believe that if I am using a person's experience as substance for a column, that person should know what I am writing about, where it is being published and who I am writing for.

The problem is that the very act of seeking consent shifts my attention from writing well to worrying about giving offence. This worry can easily translate into showing people or situations in an inauthentic (usually unduly positive) light. Such writing quickly loses its charm and integrity.

Therefore, I strive to develop alternative ways of incorporating stories that don't require explicit consent. In doing so, I have learnt from other doctor-writers to write 'composite' stories based on individual events. There is a core idea supported by snippets of details from various encounters to make the story whole but not exclusively that of one person. Generally, this achieves the balance between writing for the public and respecting individual privacy.

I sometimes jest that every patient is a potential story, but I am clear that first I am a doctor to my patients. Illness and vulnerability are not things to be exploited but there is a case, and even an obligation, for doctors to tackle societal issues. Within healthcare, issues that never go away are accessibility, insurance, cost and communication.

Fields such as climate, finance, education, construction and transportation will present their own opportunities to weave individual experiences into the big picture.

In my experience, the trouble is rarely the inability to discern the need for consent; the gap is between knowing and acting. Just because people have bigger worries than finding their experience reproduced in a column doesn't absolve a writer of the responsibility to be ethical.

When I seek consent, I keep the explanation simple and truthful.

I identify what aspect of an experience made me think again, why I want to write about it, and how it could help others.

I assure people of their privacy, and always give them time to consider my request, emphasising their right to say no. I make it especially clear to patients and relatives that their refusal will not affect our therapeutic relationship (but I do take care to be selective when asking in the first place).

The surprising thing is that hardly anyone says no. People want to share a positive story and, if they endured a hardship, are motivated to spare others.

Even when consent is not required for work in the public domain, I like to let professionals and academics know when I am linking to their work. I know from my own friends in academia how hard it is, and how gratifying, to have one's life's work reach a general audience.

When far-flung readers exclaim, 'This is exactly what happened to me!' I am relieved at achieving my goal of balancing writing with protecting privacy. The usual response from those whose experience has inspired a column has been one of satisfaction at helping others.

Today, my friends, colleagues and even patients send me ideas for future columns. Last year, a doctor friend saved me a voicemail she had received from a medical board that was investigating her for an unfounded allegation. 'There is a column in this,' she said – and there was. After the stressful matter ended, I wrote about the harm done to doctors and by extension, to society, by vexatious complainants, an uncommon notion in the public consciousness.

Modern life and work give the observant writer countless interesting subjects to explore. Writers have a duty to be respectful and responsible, and of course, readable. Adhering to some core principles ensures respect for people's autonomy and agency. I can't overstate the generosity of people willing to offer their experiences for public benefit. Seen in this light, seeking their consent feels less onerous and more community-building.

A good rule of thumb is that if your gut says you need consent, then get consent. Here, it is always better to seek permission than ask for forgiveness.

TIPS

1. Find at least one enthusiastic supporter of your writing.
2. Look for the common story in different experiences.
3. Always protect people's confidentiality.
4. If your gut says you need consent, then get consent.

Groundless complaints can drive doctors away. Here's why patients need to be held accountable

Of course we must provide a high standard of care. But a broken grievance process can do harm

19 June 2024

Guardian

We have heard all about accountable doctors. Here's why patients must be held accountable.

'I saved you a voicemail,' my friend says over a hastily arranged lunch. After ordering, I hit play and listen not once but three times. The message is like a poorly microwaved meal: warm on the surface, stone cold inside.

The caller is the Australian Health Practitioner Regulation Agency, the authority that ensures the public can maintain trust in the medical profession.

In the message, a man politely conveys that a complaint against my friend is on the way. Acknowledging that this can be stressful news, he urges her to avoid stress although he doesn't suggest how she might do so amid the mystery surrounding the notification.

She spends the night terrified. Unhappy and malcontent patients from 25 years of practice race through her mind. In the habit of apologising and fixing things, did she offend someone so grievously that it triggered a complaint?

The next morning, after a distracted drive, she sees patients she could not bear to cancel. When her inbox pings, she waits until the last patient has left. The email states that she is under review and gives her two weeks to respond. Adding insult to injury, she must list all her workplaces, so the public is shielded while she is investigated.

The complaint is surprisingly superficial. A patient has accused her of missing a diagnosis of chronic pain, correctly diagnosed ten years later, and questions how she could have missed it.

My friend's first reaction is that she cannot remember that patient. A search of her database reveals no such name, which instead of relief triggers dismay. Why should a patient go amiss? Was the database lying?

She drives home late at night, hungry and tired, tells no one and crawls into bed for the first of many disrupted nights' sleep.

The next day she upturns archived records from the last decade. Still nothing.

Perplexed, she finally calls AHPRA, apologising that she doesn't believe she knows the complainant.

The response is strange. A polite man says she could be right, but for good measure, assuming it were her patient, she should explain to AHPRA how she would have managed his pain.

This suggestion makes a mockery of patient care. Chronic pain is as hard to bear as it is to treat, the treatments as abundant as the causes. How could a doctor blindly answer how she would treat a hypothetical patient?

Despite her eagerness to close the matter, she finds the advice so outlandish that she calls her medical insurer. Her lawyer drafts a curt response to AHPRA saying no thanks.

But then her expectation of a swift resolution is thwarted by an uncertain wait as the regulator and the Medical Board of Australia study the case.

Meanwhile, anxiety erodes her equanimity.

Why would someone target her? What if the regulator unearths some other wrong? Could she lose her licence? And if not her licence, then her reputation? If she loses her livelihood, who will pay the mortgage and school fees?

It is impossible to prevent the disillusionment from seeping into her attitude. She disengages from seemingly nice patients, wondering who else will complain. Having barely taken maternity leave and sacrificed many family occasions to serve the community, she kicks herself over a thankless job performed at personal cost.

But the best doctors only *imagine* caring less, they never really stop caring. By day, she fulfils her duty to patients, consistently overbooking and overworking. At night, she loses sleep and peace of mind.

AHPRA advises doctors under investigation to talk to their friends in the same boat but, sadly, they too have tales of woe.

Like the story about my cancer patient who repeatedly declined appointments. My pleas to see me (or someone else) were matched by her refusals. Then, she became incurably ill and complained that I had been negligent. My empathy collided with a proverbial slap in the face; the burden of proof fell on me.

Doctors fear that until they are exonerated there is no knowing how even the most baseless complaint will turn out. The only consolation I can give my suffering friend is that she is so good that other doctors choose to see her.

The power imbalance between doctors and patients, and the egregious harm that some patients suffer at the hands of a few doctors rightly means that all doctors should be held to a high standard of care. But it's a broken system that holds doctors accountable but not their patients.

AHPRA says vexatious complaints account for less than 1% of notifications. Doctors challenge this, with a poll of 1,290 GPs showing that 80% believed they had been subjected to such a complaint.

Patients have registered complaints for being refused a script, disability certificate or medical leave and for being asked to wear a mask in the waiting room. Every complaint takes hours of paperwork and months of dread to refute.

Doctors worry that AHPRA's vexatious notifications framework may not be working as it should.

Why this matters to society is that groundless complaints cause sufficient psychological harm to drive doctors away, leaving entire communities without sound medical care. Which is why complaints should be fact-checked and triaged, complainants must be educated about their responsibility, and doctors should not be made to feel prematurely guilty.

After months of uncertainty, AHPRA tells my friend to relax, there is no case to answer because she had told the truth. She'd love to know what consequence the patient faced for making a seemingly unfounded accusation and how other doctors might be protected from her experience.

My friend absorbed the cost and the angst. But next time she might just quit, and we would be left lamenting that, when the complaints process is flawed, the patient wins nothing, and the community loses a good doctor.

About this column

This is an instance of paying attention to a chance event and spotting the writing opportunity in it. Doctors typically enjoy greater power than their patients, but complaints are a chance to reverse the status quo.

This is why legitimate complaints should be encouraged and the outcomes published when they are in the public interest. However, frivolous, ill-founded and vexatious complaints are costly for doctors and broader society when hassled doctors retire early.

My friend was not alone in feeling aggrieved; the real-life description of how one unwarranted complaint can ruin a doctor's reputation and finish a career resonated with many professionals, who discussed their experiences of having been unfairly treated by the authorities.

Following the column, my friend and I were interviewed by various media outlets, thus extending the life of the topic. By the end of the year, an independent review (which had been underway) was published of the vexatious complaints management process and the regulatory body accepted its recommendations.

I enjoyed navigating the tricky terrain of planning and writing this column. Debating a sensitive topic fairly but firmly helped my close friend and advocated for the medical profession.

What to Know About Sharing Personal Details

'Fill your paper with the breathings of your heart.'
William Wordsworth

'You can see them if you want.'

I know the midwife meant it kindly, but still, her words got under my skin. They are not exhibits, but human beings of potential, I retorted silently.

That day, my body had rejected not one but two beings. I had returned to Australia after a successful Fulbright year in Chicago and a blossoming twin pregnancy. All my appointments had been seamless and I remember my Indian obstetrician beaming along with me at the sight of the tiny fluttering beings on her ultrasound screen.

Then, at my very first obstetrician visit in Australia, I discovered that the twins had developed, and were dying of a condition mentioned in the fine print of textbooks. Days later, they really were gone, but my bewilderment was still building. How did it happen? What did I do? What happened next?

It's remarkable how a troubled mind finds new ways of meting out more punishment. My capsized pregnancy reminded me of another failure: when I was learning to drive, I kept failing my driving test due to silly mistakes that no one else made.

What to Know About Sharing Personal Details

So, while my friends were effortlessly getting their driver's licences, I encountered a humiliating wait. The same applied to swimming. Since we didn't have any pools when I was growing up in India, I never got the hang of swimming despite adult lessons. In a sports-mad country like Australia, everyone swam. I didn't know anyone like me.

I squirmed at the irony that a young, healthy, outwardly successful person like me should stumble at the things that were second nature to other people.

My thoughts travelled immediately to my cancer patients processing their shock diagnosis. 'I had no idea there was anything wrong.' 'They detected it on a physical for my work.' 'My hand just landed on the lump.' Instead of treating the people who said these things to me, it was my turn to be treated.

The young midwife was memorably kind. A mother to two young children herself, I could sense that she felt the pain of caring for a 'potential' mother to two children.

'So, what do you think?'

I knew she meant well and probably didn't want me to regret a rash decision but, in that moment, I resented her presence and all that it signified: healthcare professional, mother, calm, collected, thoughtful – all the things I wasn't.

Even though my mind was running to a hundred places, I was sure about one thing: I would experience my first taste of motherhood as a joyous rite rather than a cruel punishment. Which meant I was not going to see the dead bodies and no one was going to convince me otherwise.

'I am okay,' I replied, turning away and pretending to be asleep. Thankfully, she understood.

Afterwards, that whole year felt stabbing and menacing. In the earliest stages of pregnancy, within the first four weeks, the overall risk of miscarriage is thought to be 25%. With every passing week, the chance of a successful pregnancy increases, so that by the time a woman is 20 weeks pregnant, the risk of loss is less than one per cent.

Having lost both the twins after 20 weeks, I was an outlier times two.

Would there ever be another pregnancy? Did every woman have to endure a quota of bad outcomes like miscarriages and in-utero deaths before encountering success? What if there was a defect lurking in my body that my doctors had failed to diagnose?

As I pondered these questions, I went back to work and treating patients.

When people eyed my swollen abdomen and asked when the baby was due, I smilingly assured the mortified ones that really, it was okay to ask, before going to the bathroom and willing my body to return to normal.

I cried at the thoughtful letters, one from my old boss and another from my obstetrician, who had been dumbfounded at finding the unexpected diagnosis on a routine scan. I tried to be resilient and imagine a different future. It was hard.

Blessedly, it was from a place of strength with three beautiful and healthy children that I watched the dawn of the ten-year anniversary of the loss of the twins. Being a pragmatic person, who dealt daily with life and death, I assumed I was over my own experience, so it was somewhat unsettling to notice a stirring within me as the date of my loss grew closer. Something in me was vying for expression, searching for a way to honour the occasion.

What to Know About Sharing Personal Details

Wordsworth advises the writer to fill your paper with the breathings of the heart. But how? I could obviously fill pages of my journal, but the real question I had begun asking myself without even knowing it was whether I was brave enough to write a column in the *Guardian*.

A journal entry doesn't demand a word count, attention to detail, parsing of emotion or even verifiable facts. A stream of consciousness to appease one's emotions might be the only medicine one needs. A column, on the other hand, must be factual, concise and balance the right amount of narrative and message. Easy reading is hard writing.

I was aware that given the sensitive subject and the public platform of the *Guardian*, there was no walking back what I wrote. So I thought about it for days, writing many versions in my head.

Finally, what made up my mind was my awareness of the doctor–patient relationship. When patients see us at their rock bottom, they can think that their doctors are immune to difficulties while of course nothing is further from the truth. I was motivated by the idea that a doctor rendering a private loss visible might go some way towards helping others.

My life-changing experience felt too monumental to confine to 900 words. It was time to follow my own rules of writing by considering a few main points.

One, I wanted to normalise the many pregnancies that ends in a loss.

Two, in rushed times, the most important thing professionals who feel helpless in the face of illness can do is to be kind and hold space for the grief.

Lastly, there is no expiry date for grief or a proper way to grieve. People deserve space and understanding. I had declined bereavement counselling in favour of writing my way out of grief and emerged stronger for it.

I spent a long time writing, rewriting and reflecting on my column before I finally hit send with more than a little trepidation. This time, I was sending out to the world a piece of myself. I think that if I had dwelt too much on what people might say, or asked others whether I should write the piece at all, the courage to relive the experience might have seeped out of me.

I remember my editor wrote back that day that she was 'humbled' to be the first person to read the piece. I didn't pay attention to the remark until the column was published and the comments flooded in. So many people shared their own or their children's account of losing a pregnancy, a searingly personal and yet communal occurrence. Their words were exclusively thoughtful, consoling and affirming, a departure from some of the polarising and harsh comments that can pass for discourse.

This column remains one of my favourite pieces of writing and was widely read. The comments still make me emotional. Many readers found the column helpful, cathartic and moving. One said she had printed out a copy for her doctor, whose bedside manner she admired. Another did so for the opposite reason. One of my correspondents was a grandmother struggling to console her son and daughter-in-law after the loss of their twin pregnancy – she sent them my column as a consolation for the future.

I felt embraced by strangers. My favourite, biased comment was this. 'If they were anything like their mum, they would have been beautiful boys'.

What to Know About Sharing Personal Details

Writing about your own experience

If you are thinking of writing for the public about a personal issue, here are some things to consider.

Writing authentically and being vulnerable can strike a chord with readers. It might also help your writing career – I know a few writers who have found broader success after publishing short pieces about a personal experience. My former classmate wrote an award-winning book after showcasing her initial writing elsewhere. However, recognise that there are other consequences.

In retrospect, I was surprised that no one at the *Guardian* thought to ask me, 'Are you sure you want to publish this?'

Now, with experience, I realise that the priorities of the publication and writer are not always aligned. Publications will happily use 'catchy' writing to catch an audience. The onus is on the writer, the person who bears the long-term consequences, to be aware.

Since disclosing a personal issue could potentially impact your privacy, employment, insurance and relationships, pause for a 'note to self'.

For instance, I did not consider the impact of the column on my family. My unaware relatives and elders might have discovered my news in an unorthodox way and been upset. Young relatives concerned about family history might have felt anxious about their own future. Inexperienced and absorbed in my own story, these implications didn't cross my mind. I would weigh them more carefully today.

Know your boundaries, recognising when, how and what to share about your personal life. Remember that people close to the event may have differing perspectives and counter your version.

Think about the potential impact of your column on people's lives and your own relationships. Seek consent where appropriate.

It is a golden rule to treat other people with dignity and respect and guard against causing harm or discomfort. Readers appreciate sincere writing that neither diminishes nor elaborates details. As much as I respect the platforms that publish my work, I would not consider them the final arbiter of how much personal revelation is enough – and neither would they want to be in that role. I am fortunate to work with editors who exercise prudence on behalf of their writers.

It is obvious that personal experiences are not universal experiences. On one hand, this is self-explanatory – of course, our personal experiences belong to us. But when we share them through writing, we want them to evoke the same emotions in others that they did in us. It can be surprising, frustrating and disappointing when this doesn't happen. Some of my most heartfelt columns are greeted by what feels like a communal shrug or the deadpan one-word response of my teenagers to my bubbling enthusiasm, 'And?'

Writers I admire advise that the key to growth and improvement is being open to critical feedback, but I know how hard this is in practice. At such times, it's important to remember why you write – to make sense of your own world; bring awareness, knowledge and, perhaps, comfort to your readers; or something else.

Not everything will (or needs to) appeal to other people as you know yourself when you make a choice about what to read and what to avoid.

Your writing becomes part of your digital footprint

The final thing to remember is that once published, your writing becomes part of your digital footprint. I still receive the occasional dig about dimly remembered things I wrote years ago.

My writing has also been scrutinised as part of being vetted for jobs. At one interview, I was even asked to explain some lines from a column taken without context. Another time, I was asked if I would stop writing if successful – I said no.

I see writing as an extension of service to society, so long as my writing illuminates issues and doesn't hurt others. I had not considered these dimensions and in truth, they have only gained relevance over a long time of writing.

A column that shares personal details has the power to move readers and make a lasting impression. Remember to be responsible to yourself and those close to you.

TIPS

1. Personal stories make for some of the most powerful writing.
2. Before sharing personal details, consider the implications.
3. When it comes to privacy, it is better to seek permission than forgiveness.

Losing my twin baby boys for ever changed the way I treat my patients

I will never know the kind of doctor I would have become without the searing experience of being a patient, but I like to think my loss wasn't in vain

15 June 2015

Guardian

Around this time ten years ago, I was poised to start my first job as an oncologist when personal tragedy visited in a way that would forever change the way I would practise medicine.

I had returned from my Fulbright year at the University of Chicago, blessed with only the joys and none of the irritations of being pregnant with twins. Landing in Melbourne, I went for a routine ultrasound as a beaming, expectant parent. I came out a grieving patient. The twins were dying in utero, unsuspectedly and unobtrusively, from some rare condition that I had never heard of. Two days later, I was induced into labour to deliver the two little boys whom we would never see grow. Then I went home.

If all this sounds a little detached it is because ten years later I still have no words to describe the total bewilderment, the depth of sorrow and the intensity of loss that I experienced during those days. Some days, I really thought my heart would break into pieces. Ten years later, the din of happy children fills our house. But what I have found myself frequently reflecting on is how the behaviour of my doctors in those days profoundly altered the way in which I would treat my patients.

An experienced obstetrician was performing my ultrasound that morning. Everything was going well and we chatted away about my new job until he frowned. Then he grimaced, pushed and prodded with the probe, and rushed out before I could utter a word. He then took me into his office and offered me his comfortable seat. Not too many pregnant women need a consultation at a routine ultrasound.

'I am afraid I have bad news,' he said before sketching a picture to describe the extent of the trouble. I thought for a fleeting moment that my medical brain would kick in and I would present him with sophisticated questions to test his assertion that the twins were gravely ill. But of course, I was like every other patient, simultaneously bursting with questions while rendered mute by shock.

I was well aware that doctors sometimes sidestepped the truth, usually with the intent of protecting the patient. I knew he could easily get away with not telling me any more until he had more information, but I also knew that he knew. I read it in his face and I desperately wanted him to tell me.

I asked the only question that mattered.

'Will they die?'

'Yes,' he said, simply holding my gaze until his tears started.

As I took in the framed photos of children around his office he probably wished he could hide them all away.

'I don't know what to say,' he murmured, his eyes still wet.

Until then, in thirteen years of medical training, I had never seen a doctor cry. I had participated in every drama that life in bustling public hospitals offers but never once had I seen a doctor cry.

My obstetrician's tears stunned me but also provided immediate comfort. They normalised the mad grief that had begun to set inside me. Yes, the doctor's expression said, this is truly awful and I feel sad too.

'You are sure?'

'There is a faint chance that one lives but if you ask me, things look bad. You know I will do everything I can to confirm this,' he said.

The obstetrician had told the unflinching truth and in doing so almost surgically displaced uncertainty with the knowledge that I needed to prepare myself for what lay ahead. I had test after test that day, each specialist confirming the worst. I think I coped better because the first doctor had told the truth.

Two other notable things happened that week. Among the wishes that flowed, another doctor wrote me an atypical condolence note. His letter began with the various tragedies that had taken place that week, some on home soil and others involving complete strangers. 'I ask myself why,' he wrote, 'and of course there is no answer to why anyone must suffer.'

Until then, everyone had commiserated only at my loss – and I was enormously grateful – but here was someone gently reminding me that in life we are all visited by tragedy. All the support and love in the world won't make you immune to misfortune, he was saying, but it will help ease the pain.

Finally, there was the grieving. I lost count of the pamphlets that were left at our door to attend support groups, counselling sessions and bereavement seminars, but we were resolutely having none of it. My midwife called me out of the blue – it was a moving exchange that taught me how deeply nurses are affected too. But I didn't need counselling, I needed time. I valued the offers but I knew that my catharsis lay in writing. I wrote myself out of suffocating grief, which eventually turned to deep sadness and then a hollow pain, which eventually receded enough to allow me to take up my job as a brand new oncologist. How I would interpret the needs of my patients was fundamentally altered now that I had been one myself.

Cancer patients are very particular about how much truth they want to know and when. I don't decide for them but if they ask me I always tell the truth. A wife brings in her husband and his horrendous scans trigger a gasp of astonishment among even the non-oncologists.

'Doctor, will he die from this?' she asks me.

'I am afraid so,' I answer gently, 'but I will do everything in my power to keep him well for as long as I can.'

It is the only truthful promise I can make and although she is distressed she returns to thank me for giving her clarity. Sometimes honesty backfires, when the patient or family later say they wanted to talk but not really hear bad news. I find these encounters particularly upsetting but they are rare and I don't let them sway me from telling the truth.

Oncology is emotionally charged and I have never been afraid of admitting this to the very people who imbue my work with emotion. I don't cry easily in front of patients but I have had my share of tears and tissues in clinic and, contrary to my fears, this has been an odd source of comfort to patients. In his Christmas card, a widower wrote that when my voice broke at the news that his wife had died he felt consoled that the world shared his heartbreak. It can be tricky but I try to put my patients' grief into perspective without being insensitive. It's extraordinary how many of them really appreciate knowing that I, and others, have seen thousands of people who are frightened, sad, philosophical, resigned, angry, brave and puzzled, sometimes all together, just like them. It doesn't diminish their own suffering but helps them peek into the library of human experiences that are catalogued by oncologists. It prompts many patients to say that they are lucky to feel as well as they do despite a life-threatening illness, which is a positive and helpful way of viewing the world.

I will never know what kind of a doctor I might have become without the searing experience of being a patient. The twins would have been ten soon. As I usher the next patient into my room to deliver bad news, I like to think that my loss was not entirely in vain.

12

Tackling Sensitive Issues

'Give every man thy ear, but few thy voice'
Hamlet, William Shakespeare

As I walked down a hospital corridor, a poster caught my attention. It was advertising 'accent reduction classes' and promised doctors and nurses a better career and upward mobility by diminishing their accent. My mind immediately went to all the foreign graduates with whom I worked and without whom Australian healthcare, like that of most other rich countries, would come to a standstill.

Half the Australian population has at least one parent born overseas, so 'foreign' accents are ubiquitous. In the region where I work, nearly every second patient hails from a different country and patients are grateful for doctors and nurses who speak Farsi, Bosnian, Cantonese, Dari, Mandarin, Tagalog and Hindi. The kind of rapport and connection this delivers cannot be achieved through an interpreter.

Good service towards non-native English speakers is not simply a matter of finding an interpreter; anyone who has been stuck in a foreign country knows the palpable relief of discovering someone who speaks the same tongue. It's common for vulnerable patients to request care from a familiar doctor and, as an oncologist, I have been able to convince patients to adhere to treatment through shared language and customs.

In a multicultural country being bilingual and retaining an accent confers an advantage. Of course, thick accents can impede communication and this can sometimes harm patients, but the message of the poster struck me as simplistic.

Recalling the accents I had heard that week, funnily enough, the one that was hardest to understand was a rich Scottish brogue, which prompted me to ask the doctor to slow down and repeat what he was saying.

But the 'lose your accent' poster only carried photos of Chinese and South Asian doctors and nurses, implying these were the people who needed changing.

Australia is a largely peaceful place but not without its pockets of intolerance and racism. In an era of confected outrage, it would have been easy to stir controversy by posting the flyer on social media. But that was not my intention; instead, I spotted an opportunity to underscore the reliance of the public on foreign-trained health workers.

As I have mentioned before, I love the idea of a challenge. After all, we write for many reasons, among them to foster inquiry and interrogate existing notions. To me, this is the antidote to boredom. However, the thought of my column backfiring on some of my own foreign-trained colleagues forced me to cool my heels.

When caught between the urge to write and a fear of reprisal, I first reflect on my own motive. Was I even slightly tempted to scold the people who put up the flyer? Admittedly, yes. But all I wanted was to provide a gentle nudge, not extract a heavy price for what was probably a well-meaning advertisement.

The message I did not want to lose is the solid contribution foreign health workers have made to society.

Tackling Sensitive Issues

I decided that I could do this with the following points.

We should not judge people by their accent alone in a country and a profession where it was essential for people to speak different languages to simply do their job. International graduates comprise a third of the healthcare workforce and are subject to instances of unfair criticism and disdain. Patients might complain about the inadequate communication skills or medical expertise of internationally trained doctors, but in my opinion, these characteristics were not limited to any one group. To tar every doctor with the same brush was unfair.

Something I thought the public might not know is that international doctors are typically posted to rural and remote areas that lack professional support or training in the nuances of culture and communication. In the same way migrant workers do the jobs that locals won't, internationally trained graduates serve places that locally trained professionals resist.

Lastly, to write meaningfully, I needed to acknowledge my own bias. Courtesy of a global upbringing, I have an 'international' accent which varies depending on my company. I have spoken with a British accent, an American twang, an Indian accent and an Australian emphasis.

Many of my patients have distinct accents which I enjoy hearing and some of my closest friends and colleagues harbour the accents of their parents' homeland. Therefore, accents are a feature of my life.

I was conscious of attracting criticism from those who firmly believed that they had been harmed by the accent of their doctor. Their stories of medical harm might reflect poorly on all international graduates. On the other hand, rural residents, in areas with less diverse populations than that of cities, saw more international doctors and might object to being portrayed in the media as ungrateful or racist.

All these considerations made me choose my 900 words with care.

I began at a natural place, by talking to migrant doctors about their perceptions. One African surgeon remarked that even before he opened his mouth, people assumed he was an orderly because he didn't 'look like a surgeon'. Another doctor recalled a patient demanding to see a 'local' but not explaining why. I myself remembered the time when a patient had openly disparaged a Chinese doctor in clinic and refused to see him. However, other migrant doctors reported no such issues and thought that patients assessed them on their clinical competence.

Next, I found patients whose doctor's accent had been a barrier and other patients who were not bothered. I realised that the impact of a strong accent depended on the kind of conversation between doctors and patients. For instance, a difficult conversation about a terminal illness required careful language and complete clarity but a fractured arm could be plastered without much dialogue. And of course, the issue cut both ways. If doctors were hard to understand, so were many patients.

I have previously quoted the Nobel laureate Thomas Mann who said that a writer is someone for whom writing is more difficult than it is for other people. It is something that I remind myself of regularly. When faced by a writing challenge that feels onerous or uncomfortable, there is a temptation to bypass it to regain comfort but these are precisely the ideas that are important to let percolate in the mind. This is the best safeguard against writing something one might regret later.

Sure enough, after setting the idea aside for a few weeks, I felt ready to write with distance and, hence, perspective. Many healthcare professionals appreciated reading an important but touchy topic and readers publicly acknowledged the foreign-trained providers who had saved their lives. For someone who is always conscious to avoid a stir, I was pleasantly surprised when this column was nominated for an award. But the most fitting conclusion was when the hospital quietly took down the accent reduction poster, never to be seen again.

TIPS

1. To grow as a writer, gradually tackle difficult topics.
2. Enrich your thinking by seeking different perspectives.
3. Thinking carefully before you write helps to limit future regret.

Accents don't hurt patients, attitudes do
In my entire medical career, I've never heard of a patient who died because the doctor had an accent

7 February 2018

Guardian

Walking up some stairs to my office, I spot a flyer stuck in a busy thoroughfare area. By the time I have absorbed its contents I want to retrace my steps to take a more careful look. Then, the onslaught of work removes all possibility of being distracted by a piece of advertising. The interpreters are overbooked today and my cancer clinic is burgeoning with people who can't wait.

The first patient is from Punjab, an elderly woman accompanied by her husband. 'What language do you feel comfortable with, English or Hindi?'

'You speak Hindi, doctor?' she exclaims, visibly relaxed. The rest of the consultation flows smoothly and she walks out feeling reassured.

A bewildered Afghan refugee looks frantically for his interpreter.

'Dari?' he asks hopefully.

'Sorry, no,' I say, before a thought strikes me.

'Bollywood?'

Recognition dawns on his face and he smiles.

'Bollywood, I like very much!'

While awaiting the Dari interpreter, we make a start in the broken Hindi he has learnt from watching Bollywood films. It's enough to build a rapport that will last years.

In the course of just one morning, the reality of Australia as a melting pot is evident as I see patients from South Sudan,

Myanmar, Cambodia and Egypt. Outside, a Mandarin-speaking nurse soothes an agitated Chinese patient and an intern talks to a pacing relative in Croatian. In the waiting room, a surgeon slips fluently between English and Greek explanations to an elderly couple.

On my way to a meeting, the flyer catches my eye again. This time, I pull it down to study it more closely. Lose your accent, the flyer proclaims, associating a foreign accent as one of the greatest barriers to becoming a successful doctor or nurse.

Invoking the spectre of failing medical qualifying exams, being constantly misunderstood by colleagues, feeling embarrassed in the workplace and even stumbling in one's personal life, it offers the services of an 'accent-reduction specialist' to demolish the barriers to a successful career in some of the best healthcare organisations in the country.

While exhorting healthcare professionals to be proud of their culture and background, it suggests a need to fit in and feel at home with the English-speaking culture in order to get that 'perfect job or that promotion'. I find this explanation naïve and I doubt that the doctor with an Irish lilt or Scottish brogue will be lining up for help.

But while my instinct is to disavow the flyer's easy premise, I am reminded of the handful of doctors I have known whose accent proved an obstacle to securing a foothold in a new country and who might have benefited from such coaching.

A colleague observes that government policy has filled the country's outer regions with foreign-trained doctors, whose language and culture differ from that of the predominantly white population. The doctors best placed to support multicultural communities work nowhere near their community; they're sent to outposts to serve out a decade-long moratorium.

'This flyer isn't for people like you. It's for those whose patients can't understand them,' he pronounces.

'Do you think their patients might judge them without giving them a chance?'

'Probably, but the patients are hardly going to change.'

Well, it's going to be hard to source doctors and nurses without some sort of a foreign accent. After New Zealand, Australia has the highest rates of foreign-born (53%) and foreign-trained (39%) doctors. One-third of Australian nurses are foreign-trained. A quarter of doctors in the United States and a third in the UK are also foreign-trained.

By 2025, Australia expects a shortage of more than 2,500 doctors and 100,000 nurses along with an uneven distribution across the country. These shortages will be increasingly met by professionals hailing from Asia and Africa, who will bring not only their professional expertise, but yes, also their accents.

For a section of these professionals, accent modification may well be a pressing matter as it can be an immediate barrier to trust, legitimacy and inclusion. But for many others, being welcomed and shown understanding and cooperation by the profession and the community they serve could prove a more promising start.

Foreign doctors and nurses understand that a vital part of their job involves communication and most take pains to improve the way they speak and engage. The flyer praises them as intelligent, educated and self-aware, which they are. They are also all too familiar with being judged by their colleagues and by society, but suggesting that erasing their accent is the straightest path to assimilation strikes me as disingenuous.

In all the years of morbidity and mortality meetings, I have never heard of a patient who died because the doctor had an accent. But I have lost count of the mishaps and deaths from inattention, overconfidence and plain arrogance. Accents don't hurt patients, attitudes do.

In business, it is recognised that diversity of culture, language and ideas benefits shareholders. In medicine, our most important shareholders are patients and I am willing to bet that in some hospital every night, a patient is alive because of a professional who is fluent in another language, and hence, speaks English with an accent.

When I was an intern, madly wondering why my Filipino patient was delirious, it was the Filipino nurse who calmly told me that he was in urinary retention. As a resident, it was the Iraqi surgeon who gave me an insight into the disproportionate distress of a refugee who had fractured a finger. As an oncologist, I entrust my patients to surgeons from Sri Lanka, Vietnam, Bosnia and Iran. Every single one has a discernible accent. Most also speak a second language, which is not so much a frill but a necessity in serving a diverse, multicultural society.

Half of Australians were either born overseas or have one or both parents who were born overseas. When patients with poor English literacy fall ill, we don't expect them to fix their accent; instead, we try to pair them with providers who understand their suffering in their language. Perhaps this is why in the public hospital I work in, patients ask to see the doctor or nurse with an accent. These doctors are successful because they kept their accent and use their hybrid identity for societal benefit.

Accent-reduction coaching claims to have helped politicians, actors and salespeople, which is probably true (although the testimonials feature only grateful-sounding doctors and nurses). No doubt, as the advertising says, the ability to hold a confident posture, nail a presentation or deliver an impactful TED Talk is attractive, but the day-to-day work of medicine is actually humble.

Good medicine involves crouching uncomfortably at the bedside so you can hear the patient through a noisy mask. It calls for a warm touch and a kind word. Good medicine is more compassionate conversation, less brilliant lecture. Committed professionals embrace dilemma and distress, joy and grief all in the course of a day. Humanity in medicine transcends boundaries of country and accent.

The last patient of the day kicks up a fuss about seeing me. Instead, she desperately seeks 'the other one with the accent'. She is Russian, old and insistent. I locate the doctor in question and the patient gives her a handsome present. When that doctor leaves, the patient placates me, 'There's nothing wrong with you, dear. But that other doctor tolerated me and my language problem on the worst day of my life, when I found out I had cancer. Who could forget her kindness?'

13

Protest Writing

'Difficulties mastered are opportunities won.'
Winston Churchill

Of the bees I carry in my bonnet, one that routinely stings is the constant mispronounciation of my name despite my best efforts to rectify this.

I was born in Canberra, Australia, where my father was an academic. My Indian parents gave me an Indian name. Unlike their friends who intended to remain in Canberra, they did not see the need for an Anglicised name that would roll off the local tongue more easily.

Ranjana is a relatively common name in India, correctly pronounced with the emphasis on the following syllables in bold – **Run**/Jna Sri/**Vaas**/tav.

We lived in India until I was ten, when my dad's job took us to the UK. It was the first time I met people who could neither say my name nor were interested to learn it.

The staff and students were indifferent. I was immensely relieved when, at the end of the year, we returned to India and I went back to my old school.

Some years later, when my dad's job took us to the United States, the problem of my name resurfaced. My first experience with American high schools was in a white, upper-crust neighbourhood.

My classmates were neither curious about a new name or a new student – although to this day, I am grateful to the teachers who couldn't say my name but taught me well.

Too afraid to correct people, I chose an education over the correct pronunciation of my name. I told myself it didn't matter; then, on every stage, cringed and bore my discomfort. But even though I was young, I disliked this attitude, especially from adults who I thought should have known better.

My thus-far benign experience created a real problem when I entered medical school. I noted for the first time that many of my Asian friends had a 'real' name and an Anglo-Saxon one for regular use. Attracted to this idea, I took on my childhood nickname given to me by my brother. It was hard to mangle a two-syllable name, Anu.

For many years, this did the trick. It was a boon to hear my name said correctly in the hundreds of interactions in class. But as I began hospital placements, another challenge arose. The hospital ecosystem was larger, made up of not just my classmates but also patients and doctors. Here, linking my nickname to my proper name was a hit-and-miss effort.

A minor inconvenience became a serious problem when I applied for an internship. During this process, one of my strongest referees, probably juggling multiple requests, wrote, 'I don't think I know this person.'

I suddenly realised why, just the previous year, a student in a similar situation had shed her nickname and insisted we call her by her proper name. Unlike me, she had anticipated the hitch. That moment was a wake-up call. When I became a doctor, I assumed my proper name.

Half of the Australian population has at least one parent born overseas and a third of the population was born overseas. Names with ethnic origins abound in healthcare.

But while I expected other people to get my name right, I couldn't help noticing what happened in the waiting rooms of the hospitals where I worked. Many doctors looked at a migrant name on their patient list and, deeming it unpronounceable, either made a token effort or butchered the name.

Why didn't they ask, 'How do I say your name?'

I work in an area of socio-economic disadvantage. My patients are often disenfranchised refugees, asylum seekers and migrants. Something remarkable happened when I took the time to study their names, gave their pronunciations my best shot and ask if I got it right – they were visibly moved. I was doing this to protect my pride but they viewed it as an emblem of respect towards them.

Dale Carnegie once observed that a person's name is, to them, the most beautiful sound in the world. I repeatedly discovered the truth of his statement in my clinic and it sensitised me to the act of generosity involved in addressing someone correctly by their name.

Enduring life with a 'challenging' name might be immaterial to some people – and admittedly, there are many bigger problems in the world – but it gnawed at me. As my writing career grew, so did my media presence. I wanted my hosts to say my name correctly, so, overcoming my reluctance, I helped every producer and host by writing my name phonetically and even practising the pronunciation with them. If they still didn't get it right, at least I knew they had tried. This felt like a minimum requirement for the effort I was putting in.

A prominent broadcaster once invited me on his live program. Despite the usual preparation, he began by mispronouncing my name. He tried a few more times, each stubborn attempt landing a progressively awful version. My embarrassment kept growing and I wished he would stop. I longed to interject with something like, 'allow me to say my name', but I couldn't find an opening and pretended to ignore the excruciating experience until the interview ended.

Later, expecting at least an acknowledgement from the producer, I was flabbergasted when he dismissed it, saying everyone knew that the broadcaster was 'a bit dyslexic'. Even if true, the explanation felt weak. I promised myself that this was the last time I would allow myself to be humiliated.

During this period, my daughter was starting high school and posed a genuine question: 'Should I change my name to make it easier for other people?'

'Of course not!' I exclaimed.

Sensitive to my own experience, I wanted her to embrace her (relatively easy to pronounce) Indian name that she likes.

'So, I correct people every time?'

'Until they get it right.'

I realised then that I would need to practise what I preached. Studying at Harvard that year, I was meeting a brand-new cohort of students and faculty. Shrugging off a familiar self-consciousness, I proactively approached my classmates and faculty, offering to show them how to say it.

This time, I noticed how people held themselves to a high standard and appreciated being able to avoid embarrassment. A behavioural economics professor (who taught nudge theory, the theory that gentle interventions can guide us to a desired outcome) did something funny – he placed a plastic figurine in his line of sight which nudged him to remember how to say my name. He said it worked!

After we graduated, a friend from my Harvard study group shared a story. She had returned to her work at a prestigious firm, where she approached a senior Indian colleague with the same name as mine and asked why she allowed people to constantly mispronounce her name. The surprised colleague replied with what everyone in her shoes knows – it was just easier.

My classmate then related what I had done, apparently inspiring her colleague to try the same approach, with success. It pleased me to hear that something I had done for myself and my daughter had had a small outward impact.

One Australia Day, a national occasion, a man of Australian Indian origin received a high honour for founding an impactful charity for disaster aid. His name and face led every news bulletin, but the reporters were consistently mispronouncing his name, even after his relatives said it correctly in the same news item.

I was perplexed. Why had no one had bothered to ask a man who had just been accorded a national honour how to say his name? I wondered if he had himself adopted a so-called 'lazy' pronunciation, but an online search revealed this wasn't the case. Perhaps he, too, had resigned himself to the situation.

When my daughter heard this, she shrugged, saying that nearly every one of her new teachers mispronounced her name after never asking her to say it for them.

This conversation was my impetus to write a protest column about an issue that had mattered to me all my life. I would use the news as my springboard to draw attention to many experiences like mine, which ranged from moments of mirth to humiliation.

This matter felt so deeply personal to me that I even wrote the headline which had lived inside my head for years. The headline felt apt in a migrant nation where many workplaces mandate cultural sensitivity training, increasingly viewed as a box-ticking exercise.

The column drew a thoughtful response, including messages from journalists who understood their role in influencing community standards.

I was satisfied to have conveyed an essential message respectfully, which aligns with my values. I was especially heartened when my daughter said that my writing had strengthened her decision to own her Indian name.

Writing has the power to bring about change

Like me, you may want to write about an issue that means more to you than others. Spirited protest writing can be an illuminating read. If it's relevant to your audience, craft your message accordingly. Drawing an emotional connection to the issue, posing a thoughtful question or advocating for change are some ways to influence readers.

As we have discussed throughout this book, choose simplicity over big words and convoluted sentences. Avoid polarising language and personal attacks; focus on the issue instead. An effective protest not only illuminates a problem but also leads to rethinking solutions.

My column validated the sentiments many people hold about their names. While it may not have been universally relevant, it held significant personal meaning for me, my daughter and many others.

TIPS

1. The observed life is excellent material for writing.
2. Know your audience to shape your message.
3. For broad appeal, focus on issues, not people.

Want to be culturally sensitive? Start by saying my name right

In a country where many were either born overseas or have at least one parent born elsewhere, there should be no place for intellectual laziness and complacency

1 February 2023

Guardian

'The best thing that happened today is one teacher asked how to say my name!' my child says exultantly on the first day of a new school year.

'And the others?'

'Oh, they don't care,' she says.

She loves her Indian name and anticipates my next question. 'And no, I didn't correct them because it's awkward, and anyway, what's the point?'

She then notes that many in the media had failed to correctly pronounce the Indian name of the newly minted Australian local hero of the year.

'It's totally cringe,' she says, deadpan.

'Cringeworthy,' I mutter, but the matter is closed.

Amar Singh, a self-described 'migrant, Sikh and true-blue Aussie', founded Turbans 4 Australia to help people facing food insecurity, notably during bushfires and floods when disaster aid is critical. In a time of polarisation and compassion fatigue, recognising Singh and the volunteers is a welcome reminder of the power of the individual to make a difference.

Now Singh will be feted across the country. And as he harnesses his newfound status to share his mission, he might reasonably decide that now is not the time to be fussy about emphasising the appropriate syllable of his name. But for his sake and the sake of all those migrants who are resigned to having their name changed, mispronounced and mangled, I hope we can accord him this basic courtesy.

Amar is a beautiful word that means immortal in Hindi. But what do you do when a name is too foreign, too long or too hard? You could ask the person to say it. Or ask someone else who knows. You could even appeal privately to Google.

Instead, Singh's teacher problem-solved by swapping his name to David.

'I know that's your name, but what are you called?' is a question I encounter too. Worse is, 'Well, with that name, I am not even going to bother', conveniently blending petulance with blame. So, throughout medical school, I used my monosyllabic childhood nickname, only to realise my error when, during my search for an internship, one referee wrote a vexed, 'I don't think I know this person.'

This was the trigger to revert to my 'real' name, and develop my own triage system of expressing polite objection to its mispronunciation.

Important and busy people (to my mind) received a free pass. You also didn't teach a dying patient how to say your name; their gratitude was enough. Healthier patients could try harder and indeed, requested it. At speaking events, I considered arbitrary factors like the significance of the occasion, whether I would be invited back and whether the host looked receptive. On radio and television, I spoke to the producer and was impressed when conscientious presenters checked with me before going on air.

Those who made the effort almost always got it right but even if they didn't, their effort was a sign of respect.

This changed one day on prime-time radio in Sydney when the presenter began by mispronouncing my name. I let it slide, trusting his producer to correct him.

His second attempt was ridiculous and grating but still, I kept quiet and focused on the interview. Then, as if trying to prove a point, he made another long and doomed attempt. He knew it but somehow couldn't bring himself to stop. I don't know what was more humiliating – his rank disregard for me or my lack of self-respect that prevented me from interjecting.

Determined to avoid a repeat, I adopted a different approach. In every new setting, from work to home, I started with, 'Let me show you how to say my name', and noted how grateful most people were. But this left the question of what to do when those grateful people felt bad when they still had trouble. I could either say it didn't matter or that it mattered so much that I'd keep helping until they got it. I first practised this during a year spent at Harvard, the same year my daughter entered high school. Encouraging her to use own her name, I figured that the intellectual giants who sought to shape my worldview could surely learn how to say mine.

At Harvard, everybody was a 'somebody' and I had to overcome my diffidence to ask that they pay the same attention to my name as I did to theirs, often joking that there would be a quiz at the end of the class. I loved that people willingly rose to the challenge, including at graduation, the time-honoured place to trip up.

This week, as Australia's local hero eloquently heralded the importance of mutual respect in a multicultural society, I was slogging through compulsory training in cultural sensitivity.

I saw all kinds of questionable exhortations but nowhere the humble advice to take the trouble to get someone's name right.

In treating patients from many different countries, I have found one way to open the door to difficult conversations is to start with an interest in their name, its origin and how they say it. Dale Carnegie recognised this when he observed that a person's name is to that person the sweetest, most important sound in any language.

In a country where half the population was either born overseas or has at least one parent born overseas, there should be no place for intellectual laziness and cultural complacency.

The next young man on his way from Punjab to Sydney should know that he won't have to change his name to David to fit in. He can be called Amar and we will learn to say it right.

14

When Writing Offends

'If I lose mine honour, I lose myself.'
Antony and Cleopatra, William Shakespeare

One of the most difficult conversations I have as an oncologist is about death and dying, something that still feels onerous after twenty-five years of practice – as I think it ought to. Every patient's end-of-life experience is different and consequential in its own way, so too every family's response. Bearing witness to how people face a universal event offers abundant opportunities for engaging with the public. Some of the columns I most enjoy writing are those that shine a spotlight on the humanity and magnanimity of people at a testing time in their lives. Predictably, these accounts elicit the warmest and most moving responses from readers, so they feel like 'safe' pieces.

But before feeling too safe, I remind myself of the times that my good intentions have backfired. Here I discuss a couple of incidents etched in my memory and offer some practical advice on how to deal with the distress when writing gives offence.

During Covid, one of my patients was admitted to intensive care. In the years we had known each other, I had finessed her treatment to achieve a very good quality of life by her own definition. She felt healthy, was taking long walks on the beach and felt optimistic about the future. I was inspired by the mutual love she shared with her husband, whom she had met at work.

About to take a sabbatical, I was anxious for her wellbeing and left detailed notes in her file. I knew that although she presented well, her body was tired and would not tolerate aggressive therapy.

On my first day back after several months, I spotted her name on the inpatient list. Having left her in good form, I fully expected to find her recovering from a minor complication and looked forward to all her news. Instead, I was shocked to track her to the intensive care unit, receiving maximal life support, her diminutive figure unconscious under bright lights, machines beeping everywhere. She was unrecognisable from the person who had given me a 'until we meet again' hug.

Her distraught husband told me that at signs of disease progression, she had been switched to an aggressive chemotherapy regimen. This standard approach in another situation had unfortunately disagreed with her. From the emergency department, she had been rushed to intensive care.

I was still digesting the news when the intensive care consultant asked if I would talk to the family about her dire status. I met her husband and children for a heartbreaking conversation: although we were doing everything possible to mitigate her multiorgan failure, her prognosis looked grim and the next twenty-four hours were critical. I was as bewildered as they were and processing the gravity of things.

That evening, on a walk to still my churning thoughts, I received a call from another intensive care doctor who apologised for the interruption and confessed that he faced an ethical dilemma.

My patient looked like she was not going to make it through the night and a Covid patient needed an intensive care bed.

Under normal circumstances, my patient would have received a 'trial of life' but peak Covid had strained healthcare resources, so the intensive care doctor was forced to preference patients with better odds of survival.

He was calling to see how I felt about moving my patient to the ward to make room in intensive care for the other patient. Instinctively, he reassured me that if I didn't agree, the Covid patient would still receive intensive care at another hospital.

Decisions to administer patients certain therapies, move them between wards and hospitals and define boundaries of care happen daily in healthcare, but during Covid, 'medical rationing' assumed a fearsome reputation. The public became wary of discrimination.

In principle, I would not admit an actively dying patient to intensive care to merely prolong suffering, but once doctors commit to such care, the patient and family expect us to honour our word. If we did not handle her dying hours sensitively her family would carry their guilt and grief into the future. Evidence shows that poorly handled deaths impact the long-term psychological health of surviving relatives. My patient's family needed to see for themselves that we had done everything possible.

I outlined these considerations to my caller, who was also an old medical school friend. I told him that he was the decision-maker in intensive care but my conscience didn't yet allow me to remove my patient from life support. However, if she deteriorated further, there was a case for moving her to the ward for palliation. I was relieved when he said he found my plan fair.

But good medicine teaches us to think of our own patient and broader society. Feeling uncomfortable at having let down an unseen patient with my decision, I was curious to know more about the Covid patient.

It was purely in this context that my friend revealed that the severely ill patient was not vaccinated and disclosed his exhaustion from caring for such patients whose unprecedented healthcare needs were proving difficult to meet.

The Covid patient was transferred out. That night, my patient died. Her bed was promptly allocated to another sick patient. This meant that each patient had received appropriate care.

Some months later, as Covid raged, and resource allocation remained front page news, I obtained consent from the family and my colleague to write a column highlighting the human toll of making on-the-spot challenging medical decisions. Unfortunately, the headline itself unleashed a mighty furore.

Columnists don't write their own headlines, so I get to see them with the rest of the world. I usually like what the editorial team comes up with – they are much better at it than me. Occasionally, I suggest a tweak and rarely, I baulk.

On this day, between seeing patients I noted the rapidly accumulating comments which predict strong engagement *and* controversy. Some people were commending the sensitive insight into a difficult dilemma and others castigating me and my colleagues for discriminating against unvaccinated patients.

Sharp emails started pouring through my website and derisive remarks lit up social media. Suddenly, I was under siege for describing what I considered a routine occurrence in the hospital. It also became evident that many people were so riled up by the headline that they didn't read beyond it. The satisfaction of a 'most read' column was soon replaced with a quiet, 'oh dear'.

As the audience figures edged close to a million, this was one time I wished the column would disappear – and this was before a hospital executive came visiting on the premise of checking to see if I was okay, but really to ensure that I didn't imperil the hospital's reputation. I could do without that sort of attention.

Reassuringly, most healthcare professionals were nonplussed by the outrage. They agreed that we made difficult decisions daily and that all the involved patients had been well cared for. But if my intent had been to underline the dilemmas of Covid, I had lost control of my message.

In the middle of controversy, it is easy to believe that everyone else has got it wrong. But amid the vociferous audience reaction, I understood that a prime factor behind the backlash was its timing. Consecutive lockdowns and ongoing uncertainty, as well as the rare but highly publicised side effects of the vaccine, had exacted a toll on public morale. The average person reading my column was not thinking rationally but responding with emotion and thinking, 'If I got sick, would a doctor deny me an ICU bed?'

That whole week, I ducked in and out of the hospital surreptitiously, hoping no one mentioned my 'viral' column. I grew apprehensive about checking email and social media. The comments accusing me of a dereliction of duty felt particularly hurtful because I consider patient care sacrosanct.

I let my angst settle and didn't respond to any commentary. It also never crossed my mind to suggest a different headline to my editors. I was happy to stand by my column.

After some days, the news cycle inevitably moved on, although even today, this column is likely to elicit a caustic remark.

What this experience showed me

Writing this column made me conscious of the worst ways in which my words could be perceived. If you want to write about an unfolding current event or controversy, my experience offers some general lessons.

It is every writer's dream to be read and discussed widely without somehow becoming the topic of conversation. Social media is a global platform that can be harnessed for good, and I have often been its beneficiary. But writing for the public can never be criticism-proof, so it pays to think through the associated challenges and risks. In what ways could your message be misinterpreted, manipulated or distorted and how might you mitigate this? How might you lose control?

Remember that people will read your writing with a different political, social or cultural lens. Knowing that the average attention time of readers is low did not stop me from assuming that they would read *my* column to the end and be reassured that my patient's comfortable death did not occur at the cost of the other patient. Where I saw care, others spotted arrogance. Where I told a human story, others detected discrimination.

When a column lands badly, a bruised ego might be tolerable, but losing professional credibility would be damaging.

Then, there is the stress of online harassment, trolling, or even a threat to life.

I have no desire to live on the edge, which brings me back to taking responsibility as a writer.

A friend and admired writing teacher has this great advice for his students that I have now committed to memory.

'Can I close my eyes and fully picture a reader and their circumstances?'

This tip, learnt late in my writing career, has helped me check myself many times.

Facts and emotions – both matter. It is certainly interesting and invigorating to write bold pieces. They are the kind of writing that encourage dialogue and debate. They help me feel alive and grow as a writer and thinker. Unfortunately, the best intentions will occasionally backfire. In that case, stop long enough to heed the lesson, then keep moving.

TIPS

1. The best-intentioned writing can (and, at some point, will) backfire.
2. When writing, ask this: 'Can I close my eyes and fully picture a reader and their circumstances?'
3. Be gentle with yourself; all publicity (and praise) eventually recedes.

My bile rises as I'm asked to move my dying cancer patient out of ICU to make room for an unvaccinated man with Covid

I understand that for a chance at survival, the Covid patient needs a ventilator, but in a career filled with ethical dilemmas, this one really tugs at me

13 January 2022

Guardian

'I don't know how you do your job' is a common sentiment oncologists hear from those who assume that treating cancer must be uniformly depressing. But this is not the whole truth. The real gratification comes from accompanying patients on a tough journey and staying the course.

Which is why I rush to intensive care when I hear that one of my long-term patients has been admitted overnight.

While I was away, her disease progressed. She had begun aggressive chemotherapy and, days later, she fell ill. Expecting a conversation about a temporary setback, I encounter a gravely ill woman who is intubated, with failing organs, on maximal life support.

Her family has been allowed in for a glimpse. Our long association makes the exchange hard. I tell them that the next 24 hours will be critical and even if she survives, there is difficulty ahead.

The misgivings have already begun – should she have had the chemo? How could a person go from working to dying in a matter of days? Did we or they miss a red flag? Her husband and children ask probing questions, but they are polite, restrained and incredibly gracious.

We're so glad you're back, the husband says. She missed you. I sense genuine affection but also the silent hope that now that I am back I will unravel the disaster. The responsibility feels enormous. Behind the masks and shields, our eyes are moist.

A few hours later, the intensive care doctor calls.

She's very unwell, he says before getting to the real point.

'I am asking you if we can make an early call to palliate and discharge her from ICU.'

'When?'

'Now.'

My disbelief must be open because it prompts the rueful explanation that a Covid patient needs an intensive care bed.

The pieces fall together instantly. With intensive care at capacity, I am being asked to move my patient to make room for another. 'After all, your patient does have incurable cancer.'

My bile rises. And even as I know it's a petty question, I can't help asking: 'Is the Covid patient vaccinated?'

'No,' he says wearily. 'That's why he is so sick.'

Recriminations flood my mind, but this is no time for argument. I have deep regard for an old colleague who feels ethically conflicted and is asking for my help. I am torn between respecting his predicament and honouring my patient.

He agrees that absent a pandemic, if I had suggested withdrawing care, he would have counselled hanging on a little longer. And he concedes that while many of my patients die prematurely, it is important for the family to know that we did all we could. To change course merely hours after our bedside conversation would multiply this family's grief. In turn, I understand that for a chance at survival, the Covid patient needs a ventilator.

'So, let's make your position really clear for the night shift.'

By nature, I seek consensus and I'd like nothing more than to relieve my colleague's obvious stress. But in a career filled with ethical dilemmas, this one really tugs at me. Only my word stands between the trajectory of a patient's life and how her family will forever recall the experience. I am staggered by a power that I never sought, and it makes me queasy.

Keeping my voice steady, I say: 'If you are asking for my permission to withdraw care tonight, I can't give it. My patient may have cancer, but she deserves a chance.'

As I worry about alienating him, his voice breaks.

'I hope that if asked, my parents' oncologist would make the exact same decision.'

The revelation leaves me speechless, but with patients to see, there will have to be another time to ask after him.

Much is being said about the courage and sacrifice of health professionals to keep the healthcare system running but almost all of us would rather be on the frontline than anywhere else. When we enter the profession, we consecrate ourselves to serving humanity – there could not be a better time to do this. From the students rolling up their sleeves to the specialists redirected to treat Covid patients, not to mention all the nurses, paramedics and service staff sustaining a threatened workforce, this is an extraordinary and privileged time to be on the frontline.

But truth be told, we will spare the kitchen orchestra and the free drinks in exchange for a genuine reckoning with the difficulties we are facing. Often, medicine, needs to fix up its own troubles. But this time, there is something every individual has the power to do.

There is strong evidence of the efficacy of vaccines in protecting against severe illness and death. Even with the more infectious Omicron variant, the fully vaccinated are less unwell and have a greater chance of leaving hospital for home.

The collective request from a concerned and tired workforce to the public is: get vaccinated, get your booster and keep up sensible precautions. No one wants to be in the invidious position of deciding whether to save you or the next patient. (Yes, rationing happens everywhere but it doesn't have to be as egregious.)

My patient died quickly in intensive care. When we spoke, her family was grateful for our compassion and care and could not fault the system.

We don't know what happened to the other patient. If he endured a prolonged wait, his family might feel let down by the delay, though his certain extended stay in intensive care will impact the next patient.

I doubt this will be any consolation to anyone, least of all those who must actually make the difficult decisions.

15

How to Navigate Criticism

'To avoid criticism, do nothing,
say nothing, be nothing.'
Elbert Hubbard

'Then there is this guy at work who says your writing does nothing for him – and I say, "Go back and read it again".'

Having recently joined a health advisory board and feeling self-important, my bubble burst when a fellow doctor casually dropped this remark after complimenting me on my writing.

Even as I smiled and feigned nonchalance, my chest tightened.

My colleague had just shared a rather touching account of how a column had impacted his own communication with a vulnerable patient, but my warm glow had suddenly chilled.

Had I grown boring? Were my columns repetitive? What if that other man wasn't alone in losing interest?

This exchange reminded me of one from my early days of writing when I became accustomed to asking a friend for feedback because it was easy. I had made the rookie mistake of assuming that to be my friend was to like my writing.

I should have detected his lack of interest long before he had reason to divulge, 'I guess I am not your audience.'

Although I was piqued by the implied criticism, he had done me a favour by imparting a lesson that I have subsequently learnt from fellow writers. Asking someone close to you to read your writing *dispassionately* is a mistake. The operative word is dispassionately: after years of writing, I understand how difficult it is for people who care about you to be unbiased about work that they know is close to your heart. Therefore, it is best not to ask.

Coping with criticism

Comment and criticism comes with the job of writing for the public. A lifetime of being a student makes me just as eager for feedback today as I was in my days of study. On the day my column is published, I enforce a complete break from thinking about writing unless there is a problem. Some days later, I like to touch base with my editor. This is a chance to find out about audience metrics, comments and criticism. When someone complains to the newspaper (instead of writing directly to me), I may be asked for my view.

The *Guardian* tag of opinion writer has never sat comfortably with me because it suggests that I should have strong convictions, which I seldom do. My days in medicine are spent climbing down from my strongly held opinions to consider every perspective. For instance, regardless of how fearful I am that for a given patient, the toxicities of treatment would be far worse than the cancer, it is the patient who must be convinced. This requires parking my view and listening to the patient, which inevitably yields perspectives that I had not considered.

So when I write, I seem to spend a lot of time doing the same: shelving strong opinions in favour of moderate expressions and different perspectives. I used to worry about not being bold enough

How to Navigate Criticism

to venture from polite persuasion into resolute opinion but a long career in oncology has been a lesson in humility.

I am fortunate that the subject matter of my columns typically elicits erudite and helpful comments. But in an era where it is easy to post reactively and anonymously, some dismissive, rude and uninformed remarks come with the territory.

For instance, when I wrote my previously mentioned column about vexatious complaints against doctors, it generated much debate. Among the measured comments about the power imbalance between doctors and patients there were many inflammatory and unfair claims directed at doctors.

Upon reading just a fraction of the comments, a doctor friend indignantly asked how I had the appetite for such discourse every time I wrote.

I mused that the plainly uninformed or disrespectful comments were annoying but, in some ways, easy to let slide. It was the tempered, considered criticism with more than a grain of truth that pinched.

As a doctor trained to care for my patients, I can't imagine causing distress through writing. After working hard at choosing my words carefully, at the bedside and in writing, it's personally disappointing to fail.

Here are some ways I navigate criticism.

First, I believe that readers have a right to disagree with me and I welcome the fact that in a busy world, they care to engage at all. Admittedly, this healthy attitude can still cause issues, especially when I sense that my professional colleagues disagree with me. However, the practice of medicine is good at drilling into doctors that their point of view is but one among many.

Learning to separate ego from work is a continuous process. I curate the tips that sharpen my insights and prompt ideas for future columns and sidestep the rest. No one likes an armchair expert; I work hard to accept criticism, acknowledge mistakes briskly and smooth things over. By closing the loop, I sleep better.

I almost never respond on social media, where we have all seen innocuous comments assume a life of their own. For one, it's time-consuming and there is seemingly no end to it, which doesn't help me improve as a writer.

Never trust a writer who claims to not read the reviews. I read every comment and email. The comments section of the column is especially interesting: here, readers will combat unfounded claims, add perspective, and sometimes expand on or defend my point. I learn a great deal from reading the comments.

I try to write back to almost everyone who writes to me personally because I appreciate the extra intention of my correspondents who hail from all over the world and have made the effort to find me. The only emails I ignore are the (rare) abusive ones.

Some years ago, when I wrote a piece decrying opioid overuse in the hospital emergency room, several readers chastised me for never having known the pain of passing a kidney stone and the unmistakable relief provided by a dose of morphine. I realised their comments rang true from the accounts of some of my own patients, who had compared the pain of passing stones to that of childbirth. I asked my editor to amend what had initially come across as an uncompromising stance.

Another time, a column about cholesterol-lowering drugs known as statins ended up sounding strident and even dismissive towards people who rejected statins. The comments showed me that I had minimised the real side effects and disincentives to taking lifelong statins and I learnt to temper my physician's fervour in favour of considering quality of life issues.

This would have been a great time to take the advice of my writer friend, 'Can I close my eyes and picture my reader and their circumstances?'

When I have spent days researching and writing a column and someone says, 'What would you know, anyway?', that also stings. This stems from a view that, as a doctor, I should stick to my lane and only write about medicine. But as a global citizen, a social being and a curious person, I don't see why. The trick, though, is to be discerning. In 2017, I wrote a column about the horrific nerve gas attacks that killed or maimed thousands of Syrians. The silent odourless killer smothered people in their sleep. The attacks were ordered by the former president Bashar al-Assad, who happens to be a London-trained medical specialist.

The disturbing images from Syria moved me to grapple with how a doctor whose training had involved helping patients could inflict such violence on his own people. My resulting column enraged many people who found me politically naïve and thought I should stick to writing about what I knew.

Except I thought I was doing just that – reflecting on a doctor's duty of care even if that doctor was now a president. This was the only time that I received a death threat. It led to some sleepless nights and introspection but the column was not withdrawn, and I kept writing.

It would be seven years before Bashar al-Assad was ousted by his own people and fled to Russia. The true horrors of his reign are still coming to light as Syrians describe the gas attacks said to be emblematic of his signature cruelty. I would write that column all over again.

Another contentious topic arises whenever I write about strengthening primary healthcare, often called the backbone of medicine, through better pay and conditions for general practitioners. This predictably generates a flurry of criticism from those who claim that GPs are overpaid and underwhelming. People unfamiliar with the many demands of primary care will probably continue to think like this. I like reflecting on the issues rather than picking fights with people, which is a good way to think about navigating all criticism.

Grace, kindness and deciding when to say sorry

When I was anxious about teaching one of my first writing classes, I ran my talk past a respected teacher. He said that the slide that made him the happiest was the one that said, 'Above all, be kind' – it was something he strived to teach his students.

I remind myself when writing (and working) to be a little kinder than necessary. And saying sorry early for my part.

Once, I wrote an article critical of the widespread practice of elderly, cognitively impaired or stroke-afflicted patients being denied thin fluids such as water and tea to prevent aspiration pneumonia, a condition where food and drink goes the wrong way down and enters the lungs. In fact, there is no good evidence that limiting fluids avoids aspiration, but the practice has a profound impact on quality of life.

Readers who had witnessed the problem applauded the column, but it offended at least one speech pathologist who viewed it as an attack on her profession.

When I first opened her email in the morning, I had a long day of patients ahead.

I was tempted to dispense with her email by typing out a terse, defensive response, something that every guide ever written about handling criticism says not to do. I picked up the phone instead.

I explained my intention to raise awareness of a common and distressing problem rather than blaming a profession and offered to give a talk to her group. She was surprised and then mollified, saying that she had not expected any response.

Medicine has taught me the value of communication in nipping complaints in the bud.

Another time, someone was deeply upset about a column I had written about his deceased relative although the patient's spouse had given his consent. My intuition told me that the relative was grieving and I felt awful for having compounded that grief. To add to the awfulness and my internal conflict, the complaint arrived after my column was nominated for an award.

Somewhat depressingly at the time, my editor was not as sympathetic as I wanted, but she was right to caution me to be extra careful when writing sensitive pieces. Yet another opportunity to ask, 'Can I close my eyes and picture my reader and their circumstances?'

This was a moment of reckoning. On one hand, I did not want to set a precedent by amending my column, a year old by that time; on the other hand, I wanted to do right by the relative.

So, in an email (which took hours of crafting and vexing), I expressed sympathy for his loss and told him that I felt terrible. I also asked what I could do to make things better. To my relief, his response was quick and conciliatory, confirming my general view that most people just want to be heard. I worked with my editor to issue a correction that made a difference to the relative without changing the gist of my column. Before recounting this incident here to help other writers, I wrote to the relative. His gracious consent and good wishes felt like coming full circle.

These examples have taught me to be courageous in writing but also quick to show grace along the way.

Check your self-importance

My happy place is a good read. The world contains so much excellent and inexhaustible writing that any individual contribution is but a speck. It's easy to note that even my best writing is noticed by very few people and even fewer care.

I can't help thinking that this one insight has instilled in me a lack of self-importance, which has been the most liberating part of my writing career. I am ambitious to write well, proud when my writing is well received, and relish the opportunities that arise from writing for the public.

But self-importance is a product of insecurity and I write best when I am not insecure.

Detaching self-importance from writing means not overthinking any external commentary, however glowing or gutting. To pause and reflect on each is the best way to improve. I am lucky to receive abundant gratitude and generosity from readers. This is certainly helpful in regarding my toughest critics with empathy and recognising that, after all, our reactions are shaped by our own experiences.

It is also important to be kind to ourselves when it comes to the internal chatter. Criticism of our work is not a measure of our intrinsic worth. Our egos are fragile things, but we should write because we have something to say in a way only we can.

Of all my self-help tools (yes, we all need them), writing, alongside exercise, is the most important. A writing habit allows me to debrief at will and invariably lightens my load even if it doesn't fix the problem. The routine of writing is salve and anchor.

It is said that the worst loneliness is to not be comfortable with yourself. While this is an entire book about writing for an audience, I have always maintained that I write first and foremost for myself. When that writing engages the public, it is the icing on the cake.

TIPS

1. With public engagement comes criticism and commentary: welcome it.
2. Take constructive feedback seriously, let go of the rest.
3. Above all, be kind.

Every Word Matters

How did we miss our colleague's grief?
Expecting to be greeted by an outpouring of sympathy, he walked into silence. When it comes to acknowledging death, all of society needs help

20 November 2019

Guardian

After decades of work and the constant demands of a busy life, a husband and wife take a trip abroad. One day they go for a walk in a national park. There, workers are doing what they do, taking care of the surrounds. Suddenly, without warning, a chainsaw goes through its final motions and a large tree comes crashing down. He walks ahead but, being a split second behind him, she is trapped and sustains severe injuries. Precious time is lost being transported by road and air to one hospital, then to another and another. Unfortunately, she succumbs to multisystem failure. Then he returns home alone. Picture his devastation. Imagine the survivor's guilt.

Back at work, a shock of a different kind awaits. Expecting to be greeted by an outpouring of sympathy at his loss, he walks into silence. People go past him and look sideways. They make an off-colour joke. Or they work with him and say nothing. His raw grief craves acknowledgment. He knows that nothing will bring her back, but a simple recognition of his loss might just pull him through the day. After all, a sorrow shared is a sorrow divided.

He is heartbroken, first at his loss, and then at the way in which that loss is unintentionally diminished by those who have known him, and them, all these years.

How to Navigate Criticism

A year from the day the tree fell, he writes a heartfelt piece about the loneliness of grieving. I am reading the paper at dawn, shaking my head in dismay at his described workplace. Who behaves like that? Where does this happen? How do people let it happen?

And then, as I scroll back up, I nearly drop my iPad in surprise because I know him. He is a surgeon from my own institution who once taught me and later cared for some of my patients. We mostly communicated via phone but from time to time we met to discuss a problem. I bite my lip. This happened to him at our hospital. From here it is only one step to a deep discomfort as I rack my brains to figure out when we last met and whether I should have had an inkling of the tragedy. Was there a circular I had missed? Did someone hold a minute's silence when I wasn't there? Worse, did he and I sit together discussing the elective surgery waitlist while he kept expecting me to say something more profound? I am mortified at the thought.

At daybreak, I call him. My heart sinks when the operator casually mentions she hasn't seen him lately. Fortunately, he answers, and my words tumble out. I am sorry for your horrific loss. I had no idea. And then, I can't resist: had I seen him in the year since the accident and simply failed to ask how he was? Gently he puts my mind at rest, saying we had neither seen nor spoken to each other lately and I wasn't to know. But it's hardly a relief to learn that while I didn't directly ignore his grief, our collective profession had and that the experience had been enough to discourage him from returning to work.

He tells me the stuff of love stories. They met on the first day of medical school and weathered the travails of training. The world respected her as an obstetrician but, more importantly, she was special to him. He enjoyed her company and had looked forward to a future with her. Nothing would bring her back but, aside from his relatives, he wanted the other important people in his life to simply say: 'I was very sorry to hear about your wife's death.' These people were the surgeons, anaesthetists, physicians, nurses, technicians, clerks and cleaners who a veteran surgeon sees more of than his own family.

But a total of three letters arrived, from trainees and secretaries. There was the odd text or email, almost begging to be ignored. From the rest, total silence. Eventually the thought of encountering that silence proved to be so powerful and decisive that he left the hospital. Better a graceful exit than shattered expectations.

He relates all this with unmistakable grace and poise, but I can't help thinking of the twin deficit to society through the untimely death of one doctor and the resulting loss of another. An experienced and respected surgeon who stops operating but mentors trainees and leads by example is a prize. If holding on to such people requires the creation of a safe space, wouldn't we want to do it every day?

It can be puzzling to think that doctors who walk countless patients through illness and mortality can be unintentionally remiss in the duty of care to their colleagues. I have no doubt that every doctor felt (very) helpless and (gratefully) guilty upon hearing the news. We witness enough random acts to know that it could have been any of us. But to translate our unspoken fears into able communication takes another leap – not so much of intellect, but rather emotion. Here we need reflection and self-correction, but I also can't help wondering whether the growing pressures of paperwork and worthless administrative tasks will make it even harder for us to find the time and the will to actively care for each other. Without each other we are nothing, but more importantly, if we aren't whole we can't help our patients either.

My first patient has arrived and now I feel a pang of regret at this inadequate phone call one year after the event. I ask mundane questions like how he spends his day and who he has meals with. Grief has a long arc and 'doing OK' is relative.

I end by saying that I was struck by the tone of forgiveness in his essay. He thoughtfully replies that when it comes to acknowledging death, all of society needs help. He is right and this is why you should read his complete essay, 'The crack of a falling tree, the terrible loss – then the silence'.

16

Seeking and Using Feedback

> 'Writing is easy. All you have to do is
> cross out the wrong words.'
> Mark Twain

When I was a budding writer, a friend asked me to read a first draft of a novel that she had poured precious hours into. The book was a satire, which is a genre I rarely read.

Had I been thinking straight, I would have explained that I was not well placed to comment on her work, but as a loyal friend who wanted to see her succeed, I convinced myself that I could provide the 'totally honest' feedback she desired. A few chapters in, I realised that while the concept held promise, its execution fell flat. The dialogue was stilted and instead of relishing the discomfort of the protagonist, as she intended, I found myself feeling sympathetic towards him and, in turn, irritated by the author's tendency to poke fun at him. My reactions did not bode well.

I was no editor or literary agent but as an avid reader, the work felt incomplete. Compounding my dilemma was the awareness that I didn't know how to provide constructive feedback about writing. In my nascent writing career, I had only encountered blunt rejection notices or, worse, silence.

Balancing the need to be truthful with the delicate task of

preserving hope felt ominously like being an oncologist. I cautiously remarked that the book could have promise if the plot were more developed and the protagonist less skewered. I helpfully added that the grammar and punctuation errors could be easily fixed with an online tool – and that she might consider sending the next version to a professional editor.

My friend did not appreciate my feedback, tartly replying that the book was not intended 'for people like you'. She was right and I should have known it. She eventually found a literary agent who couldn't convince a publisher. Like many manuscripts, this one was retired to a bedside drawer.

I felt bad but would have felt worse offering false praise. My friend never went back to her book and later reflected that writing had been a temporary filler during a dry phase of work.

Some years ago, another friend asked me to endorse a self-help book he had written after resigning from a conflict-riddled workplace. I was happy to read his book but had trouble understanding a lot of the content which strayed into philosophy. I told him honestly that I didn't feel qualified to comment and knew that he felt let down. He ended up publishing his book and finding appreciative readers but our relationship cooled for some years before recovering. From this, I learnt to be more discerning in both offering and seeking feedback.

How to accept and use feedback

It took me time to adjust my own sources of feedback. While training as an ethics fellow at the University of Chicago, I was allowed to audit a fiction-writing class taught by a popular fiction author. Each week, students brought a section of their writing for peer review. With time on my hands and hope in my heart, I wrote madly every day until it was my turn to be read.

I was eager to hear what the class thought of the first chapter of my first-ever fictional story about a woman who finds out about her terminal illness and flies to a secluded island. The dozen students read quietly until one voice broke the silence with a perplexed, 'This reads just like a real-life medical drama.' The whole class nodded. I was advised to either take a fresh shot at making my work more fictional or channel my energy into non-fiction. The honest response forced me to consider two things: what I wanted to write about and the style I wanted to use. I finally decided that narrative non-fiction was my strength. Twenty years later, I remain grateful to my class for this insight, although I haven't entirely given up on the idea of writing fiction one day.

When I was a brand-new writer, I ran my work past the same one or two people because it was easy, and they were obliging.

One person liked everything – the way we respond with emojis to text messages when we are feeling lazy. This was neither flattering nor helpful and I yearned for more. In contrast, my other reader always seemed a bit unimpressed, even if the writing he felt lukewarm about went on to be published in reputable places. It was difficult to extract any meaningful feedback from him and I glumly acknowledged that I would never appeal to his taste.

Writing isn't playdough. It is not meant to be endlessly shaped to please everyone, which means deciphering our audience and writing for people who appreciate our perspectives and engage with our writing. For many years, my old medical school professor was my sounding board. A renowned scientist and inveterate writer who was always working on a talk, paper or book until the final years of a long life, he took a genuine interest in my writing and was instrumental in bringing my ideas to life. A lifelong lesson I learnt from him was to always have a writing project on hand, no matter how slowly it evolved.

However, it wasn't until I began submitting essays to the *New England Journal of Medicine* that I discovered the power of seeking feedback from people who didn't know me, didn't owe me their loyalty, and whose job involved saying no more often than yes. I loved the challenge of reaching the *Journal*'s high expectations and always marvelled at seeing my unpolished pieces transformed into fluent works in the hands of my editor. I savoured this education as much as I loved being published in the *Journal*.

It was an altogether different challenge to pitch a book idea to a commercial publisher whose interest was based on a hard assessment of the economics. Through some acceptances and many rejections, I learnt to ask these questions from a publisher's perspective: who will sell my book? Who will buy my book? Who is my competition? How will I gain readers?

These questions hold good lessons for any type of writing. To improve, seek input from people you trust and who have the interest, insight and time to give considered feedback. If you need to take a writing course, of which there are far too many, spend time finding the right course for you. Ask the right questions first and then talk to students and faculty.

In writing this book, I have benefited enormously from quality writers who gave up their time to read my drafts with a discerning eye. These readers asked me for a deadline and said no if they couldn't do justice to it, thus demonstrating seriousness of intent.

This part of the writing process is a communal act. I pay it forward by making time to read the work of other writers and offering helpful feedback. This is not a favour but a responsibility.

This is a good place to mention that reading other people's writing is a great way of improving as a writer. It's interesting and instructive to get a glimpse into the drafts and iterations, laments and wins of fellow writers.

While writing this book, I had an opportunity to help a good friend envision his first book. Heeding my own advice, I avoided reading his manuscript until it was nearly finished but helped him find a freelance editor.

When he complained that he couldn't bear to read his writing, I told him I felt the same. It was a good way to discover that the exhilaration and laments of writing were mutual.

Asking for feedback

If you are a new writer wanting feedback, consider the following.

You need not wait until your writing is complete to seek comment and advice.

Indeed, there are different benefits to be gained at each stage of writing and some readers may serve one purpose better than another. The first round should focus on the big picture while later feedback can scrutinise word choice and turn of phrase.

Take care that the feedback you get motivates you to keep going instead of hindering progress.

Ask people you can trust to be honest *and* constructive. For instance, tell them you want to know if your writing doesn't hit the mark but also how to improve it. Conversely, if your writing is appealing, understand what aspects work so you can use them again.

Seeking and Using Feedback

Think of the people in your life who like to read. They need not be subject matter experts; in fact, a good rule of thumb is to avoid experts when writing for the public because your aim is to be understood by the general reader.

My avid reading friends typically help me right the balance between facts and storytelling and provide a great service by recommending good writing that I may not otherwise read. My editor looks out for potential pitfalls and legal tangles, although sometimes this leads down a path of rejection.

Finally, when it comes to feedback, more isn't better. Excessive commentary can be just as off-putting as a lack of engagement. Suggestions to rework the entire writing risk losing sight of the fact that the work is meant to be yours, told in your voice. The most valuable feedback is concise, thoughtful and one that opens an avenue for self-improvement.

It is worth repeating that when asked nicely, most people are willing to help and feel good about their contribution to public discourse. Remember these people, thank them graciously, and include them in your world even when you stop needing their help. This win-win situation multiplies the joy of writing.

TIPS

1. Helpful feedback is concise, thoughtful and motivates improvement.
2. If you ask nicely, most people are willing to help.
3. Treat those who help you with grace and gratitude.

An Indian dilemma

26 July 1997

Lancet

Bhagalpur, Bihar, India
2200 h, Dec 4, 1996

I stand by the bedside, holding his hand as he writhes in pain. In the dim candlelight, I notice his bare feet, hardened by years of walking unprotected through sun and rain, his hands callused, scarred and capped by black nails, his dirty torn kurta, and old khaki pants. I take in the agonised look on his face, the trickle of blood at the corner of his mouth where he has just bitten his lip.

I am in the private clinic of Dr Jha, on an elective in India at the end of my fifth year of medical school at Monash University, Melbourne, Australia. Dr Jha is still working in his office so we sit down for a chat. That is when Mr Lal is carried in by his wife and brother.

In whispered conversation with his wife, she tells me how Mr Lal was pulling his rickshaw when he suddenly felt a pain in his abdomen. Fortunately, he had been close enough to return home, where he collapsed. His brother and wife had taken him by rickshaw to the local hospital, only to find that the power supply had been cut off, there was a shortage of medications and equipment, and at that time of night help was unavailable. It is now three hours since the pain began. Dr Jha diagnoses acute cholecystitits, prescribes analgesia, and admits Mr Lal to the clinic for a cholecystectomy.

0830 h, Dec 5, 1996

Mr Lal is third in line for theatre. He looks curiously at the young man lying on a table in one corner of the room who is making choking sounds. The young man was first on the morning's list and is recovering from the anaesthetic in a room that serves as theatre and recovery room. As soon as he climbs on to the operating table, Mr Lal's eyes are covered with a piece of cloth, so that he does not see Dr Jha finishing a hernia repair. Mr Lal is given an injection and begins to feel drowsy. The anaesthetist, watching the second patient, walks to Mr Lal and intubates him. An attendant undresses Mr Lal and paints his abdomen with iodine.

Having finished the hernia operation, Dr Jha quickly makes his way to his room where other patients wait to consult him. The restless crowd spills into the consulting room. The attendant attempts in vain to admit only one patient at a time. Finally, the attendant and the crowd reach a compromise; while Dr Jha sees one patient, another lies down on the second examination table, and the others sit on a bench inside the room. A woman complains of a history of peptic ulcer. Dr Jha would like to send her for an endoscopy but knows no such facility is available, so starts her on a course of medication to stabilise her condition.

Raj, a four-day-old baby, has not urinated since birth. Dr Jha gently refers his distraught mother to a paediatrician. Nina is 21 years old and has a breast abscess. Dr Jha tells her he will operate on the abscess in the morning, notices her blanched look, rightly guesses her fear, and reassures her that it is not cancer.

I suddenly notice an old schoolfriend sitting across the room from me. She unwraps her scarf to reveal a large dressing on her neck. A recently drained tuberculous abscess discharges pus. While Dr Jha examines her wound, our eyes meet. I am embarrassed to meet her under such conditions and leave the room. On returning, I ask Dr Jha whether clean and well-nourished people can get tuberculosis; the sight of a schoolfriend with tuberculosis has shaken me, as if I expected all those who I know to be free from disease. He replies that tuberculosis is very common throughout India and no one is spared.

One of the theatre staff arrives to tell Dr Jha that the theatre is ready for Mr Lal's cholecystectomy. The rest of the throng outside must wait, most of whom have travelled long distances, many on foot, to seek treatment here. Word has spread far about Dr Jha, who, after finishing at the top of his medical class, went to the UK for specialist training and then returned to India. He cares for his own people. At least half the waiting patients will have a non-surgical complaint, but in India there is no medical system to channel patients to appropriate specialists. Dr Jha is first a general practitioner and then a surgeon, as well as physician, paediatrician, obstetrician, and gynaecologist when needed.

Dr Jha rolls up his trousers and shirt sleeves, discards his tie, scrubs up, dons a sterile gown and gloves, and walks into theatre. There is a combination of clean and unclean, qualified and unqualified in the theatre. Although the surgeon wears a sterile gown and uses autoclaved equipment, there are six other people present in civilian clothing. The ward is next to the theatre and the attendants walk freely between the two areas. The theatre door is wide open and one of the ubiquitous houseflies finds its way in; someone reaches quickly for the Baygon spray, filling the room with its intolerable smell.

Seeking and Using Feedback

The anaesthetist has been working in this clinic for the past three years. Before his arrival, a man with no medical background, personally trained by Dr Jha, carried out all anaesthetic duties, and he still assists when the anaesthetist is unavailable. The other attendants, all without medical training, are familiar with different antibiotic regimens, the various intravenous solutions used, and the general care of patients. This clinic works 365 days a year. Thousands of patients go through its doors, and they share between them just three medically qualified practitioners.

There is a cauldron of hot water beside the operating table where Mr Lal lies. Dr Jha uses the hot water to wash two large swabs during the operation. He never uses more than two swabs for fear of leaving one behind in the abdomen. There are no special staff to keep count of the equipment. The power supply fails suddenly in the middle of the operation. Someone immediately appears over my shoulder with a powerful torch until another attendant switches on the alternative power supply, a familiar routine in this power-starved state.

Dr Jha is relaxed and amiable during the operation. At the age of 63, his so-called retired life is busier than his years as Head of Surgery at the local hospital. He begins each day at 0400 h with a brisk 90-minute walk and finishes work at 2100 h. He works tirelessly, with amazing grace and confidence. There is silence as he isolates the common bile duct. Twenty minutes later, Dr Jha deftly removes the gall bladder and takes the opportunity to explore Mr Lal's intestines for signs of tuberculosis. He decides not to remove Mr Lal's appendix. If feasible, Dr Jha removes the appendix prophylactically because most of his patients are too poor to seek immediate attention if they suffer an attack of appendicitis. In a few more minutes, the incision is sutured. Mr Lal is taken aside to recover from the anaesthetic while Nina, the girl with the breast abscess, timidly arrives.

0700 h, Dec 6, 1996
I accompany Dr Jha on the ward round. We check on Mr Lal. There are ten beds in the room; no curtains separate the beds. The patients share two bathrooms. Two or three family members attend to each patient because there is a shortage of nursing staff. They sit on the bed, others on the floor; there is little space for chairs.

Mr Lal lies in bed with his wife beside him. Dr Jha smiles, takes his hand and asks him how he feels while he inspects the dressing. Mr Lal complains of pain. He is reassured that some pain is natural after surgery but it will diminish. In the meantime, he should try to walk a little and not rely heavily on painkillers. Dr Jha tells Mrs Lal not to spoil her husband just because he has had an operation. Her worried face breaks into a girlish giggle and she nods vigorously. As he recuperates, Mrs Lal buys the prescribed drugs every day so the clinic staff can administer them to her husband.

0800 h Dec 14, 1996
As I walk in, I notice that Mr Lal's belongings are packed up. He had to bring his own bedding and utensils for his nine-day stay in the clinic. The rickshaw puller's meagre resources have been almost depleted by the cost of the surgery and drugs. He must also pay for the dowry and wedding of his adolescent daughter. He haltingly tells the doctor of his situation. Dr Jha, without a moment's

hesitation, scribbles a large red F on the discharge sheet, telling Mr Lal he does not have to pay for his care. The next moment, Mr Lal and his wife are on their knees, touching Dr Jha's feet in gratitude, calling him a godsend, beseeching the heavens aloud to bless this man who has just waived his fees of thousands of rupees. I follow the couple's shadows into the distance as they walk away, Mr Lal with a spring to his step. I turn back with a lump in my throat, speechless.

This is the miracle of medicine in Bhagalpur and all over India. Even the poorest man has a chance of some relief from suffering. Unaware of the full potential and sophistication of medicine, all Mr Lal knows is that he is a man free of pain. For what good are the drugs and equipment of modern medicine if they are unaffordable, unavailable?

1400 h, Jan 5, 1997
Six weeks of my elective have passed and I leave the clinic for the last time. Some of the staff believe that they will see me in India in a few years' time, others are convinced that once I have gone to a country of comfort I will have no reason to return. I struggle in an effort to resolve this dilemma. Do I look the eager, honest faces in the eye and assure them that of course I will come back because India is my home? Or do I admit my reluctance to leave the comforts and conveniences of life in Melbourne?

My mind flashes back to Mr Lal, in excruciating pain, then to my parents, who also live in Bhagalpur. I am uneasy at the thought of my parents ever needing medical care in this city. I am consumed by the conflict. I hear Dr Jha's grim words 'superimposed on every disease here lies poverty and malnutrition', and feel an urgent desire to escape from this inadequate healthcare system, the burgeoning population, the suffocating heat and dust. Yet something within pulls me powerfully to the people of India. How would I ever be able to come to terms with my conscience if I decide never to return? Not only am I unable to promise my parents, friends and the clinic staff that I will return to India, I cannot even promise myself.

Melbourne, Australia
0100 h, Jan 13, 1997
In Melbourne, I wine and dine with friends I have not seen for many weeks. I adopt all the luxuries life affords me with natural ease. Yet, in moments of quiet, I grapple with the issues of my identity and future. I write in my journal, hoping that the path ahead will suddenly become clear. Never far from my mind is the eternal, unanswered question: am I my brother's keeper?

About this column

This was my very first published essay from when I was a medical student. I include it here as a tribute to my professor, Roger Short. Professor Short was the first person to teach me to write with authenticity and humility, to teach me to not be afraid to ask questions to which I didn't have all the answers. There is no line or sentiment in this essay that doesn't bear his impression.

In the pre-internet era, he lent me his fax machine to submit this essay. When it was published, he posted a copy of the *Lancet* to me with a handwritten note, both items I still treasure. In his note, he hoped that this essay was only the beginning of a rich writing career. Happily, he lived to read, relish and edit a lot more of my writing until he died in his nineties. But he would often say that this first essay of mine was his sentimental favourite.

My second wonderful memory of this essay is that Dr Jha's son, also a doctor, found himself reading this essay in the UK and slowly recognising that it was about his dad. It must have been a proud moment for father and son.

17

Why You Need an Editor

> 'Your manuscript is both good and original,
> but the part that is good is not original,
> and the part that is original is not good.'
> Samuel Johnson

Susan Sontag wrote that a writer is someone who pays attention to the world. I agree wholeheartedly, but finding inspiration isn't easy and the road from contemplation to action is hard, not to mention riddled with self-doubt.

I spend hours wondering what to write when I could take my own advice and start writing. When working on a book, there are months when I can't bear to read my own work and stall my own progress.

Enter a good editor, whose job it is to help distinguish good from original, motivate and empower, and turn your writing into a better version than you had imagined. I was recently co-teaching a writing class with an experienced editor who advised the students that an editor can be anyone, including a colleague who will read your work and give useful feedback. In contrast to academic or grant writing, where expert input is desirable, the ideal person to comment on writing that is meant for the public is a non-expert because it is that person you need to engage.

Like many writers, I owe enormous debt to the people who

work behind the scenes to polish my work. Here, I share some of their best advice.

Writing to a word limit

Writers are often advised to not worry about the word count but aim for a first draft. Writing begets more writing and before long, there is at least something to edit.

For practical purposes in a busy life, I like to keep in mind whether I am writing a 900-word column or a 5,000-word speech. It would be a waste of time to constantly write twice the amount only to lose half.

We have all heard of writers who discard entire drafts and show saintly patience over years, even decades. The ability to sustain attention and interest for so long is impressive but most of us must move briskly. For those pitching to a publication, disregarding the word limit is likely to result in their work never being read.

Over the last few years, my editors have become more exacting about my word limit, a challenge that I am happy to embrace.

In writing a column of 900 words, I aim to exceed the draft by no more than 150 words. Since I have deeply felt so much of what I write about, I can be hawkishly protective of every word. But good editors have shown me how this attitude is anathema to polished writing. So, if the choice is between being my own ruthless editor or letting someone else decide what to cut, I prefer to control my message and protect my credibility.

Working with editors

Aside from the few weeks auditing the fiction-writing class at Chicago, I have never attended a writing course or retreat, which

I would have relished had there been time between medical training. So, my education as a writer has been through observing how editors edit.

The person who has transformed my writing is the long-term essay editor of the *New England Journal of Medicine*, Debbie Malina. Founded in 1812, the *Journal* is the oldest continuously published medical journal in the world. Every week, it publishes a mix of critical research and thought-provoking essays and perspectives. In a world awash with publications, the *Journal* remains essential reading for many.

In December 2005, having arrived back in Melbourne with the affirmation of the Chicago faculty echoing in my ears, I answered a call in the *Journal* for writers on topics of societal importance.

For consideration, I submitted an essay about my experience of being a volunteer doctor at a refugee centre in Melbourne.

Debbie responded that although my experience did not match their need for a reporter, she found me to be a 'strong, thoughtful writer' and invited me to submit an essay for 'possible use' in the Perspective section.

Many readers consider this the best part of the publication. I had grown up admiring the essays of doctors who have gone on to achieve writing acclaim.

Looking back, her response was cautious and nowhere resembling a promissory note, but Debbie's compliment gripped me and was the fillip I needed to submit my first essay to the *Journal*. I still get goosebumps thinking back to the day it was accepted and distinctly remember opening my print copy of the *Journal*, seeing my name in print and receiving a call from an old boss to congratulate me on the achievement.

Why You Need an Editor

Publishing in the *Journal* is somewhat of a holy grail for doctors. At prestigious medical conferences, doctors will introduce their research by mentioning a concomitant publication in the *Journal*, the ultimate badge of honour.

For me to have crept in with an essay seemed unreal but what astonished the new writer in me was Debbie's editorial alchemy. When I compared my original manuscript to the revised manuscript and then the final copy, I could only marvel at its transformation. The fact that she was not a doctor meant that she had an eye for arcane words, jargon and redundant writing, the latter being the wont of every self-absorbed writer.

Debbie didn't put words into my mouth (or manuscript). She treated my work with objectivity; put keen questions in the margins to draw out my intent; suggested apt words to capture a sentiment more faithfully; suggested ways of stating a strong opinion more delicately, and skilfully juxtaposed fact with feeling.

In doing so, she made my writing come alive.

Like many authors, I find it excruciating to look at my own work, but once Debbie's eyes had gone over my essay, I found myself soaking up all the deft ways in which she had shaped it.

In the beginning, I was almost seized by moral turmoil. The edited version sounded too good to be mine.

But after working with her some more, I saw that the stories happened to me and the reflections were mine; as a different kind of expert, Debbie had brought her editorial skills to enhance my work.

Learning from the editing process

I had so much faith in Debbie that whenever I received her suggestions, I would just hit 'accept all changes' and return the manuscript. But I began making real progress when I paused to absorb the rich learnings, the most important of which was continuous self-improvement.

Instead of being deterred by the *Journal*'s prestige and rigour, I treated the editorial process as my free private tuition. For every submission that was 'tentatively accepted' (pending final approval by the editor-in-chief), I spent an hour or two dissecting Debbie's advice.

I placed my manuscript next to her edits and took mental notes about the changes she suggested. Some I didn't mind, others I loved. I saw how a turn of phrase here, a substituted word there, changed the contours of my writing and made it more pointed and eloquent. Debbie also taught me when to seek consent and when to leave out the most sensitive details to convey a message without compromising patient privacy. Slowly, but I am glad to say, surely, my style developed and my confidence grew.

With every essay that Debbie edited and the *Journal* published, I felt more fervently committed to writing. For a writer, there can be no greater gift.

I like to say that the *Journal* keeps me honest, which is the reason I have a goal of publishing one essay in it every year. Given the volume of submissions, and hence the high chance of writing for rejection, this goal is the right fit with my other commitments.

As one of the millions around the world who has grown up reading and respecting the *Journal*, I was thrilled when Debbie compiled a collection of my essays some years ago. The essays revealed some of the moving facets of human nature, social norms and the institutions that doctors like me navigate in caring for our patients.

I am proud to have maintained our continuous publishing relationship and still read the *Journal* every week for examples of good writing burnished by Debbie's editing.

I write for the *Guardian* throughout the year, filing a column every two weeks.

At the *Guardian*, I am fortunate to work with excellent editors and sub-editors, who perform different functions for every column I write.

They ensure that my writing is relevant to the public and cogent.

They also keep a close eye on what might unintentionally offend or distract from the main idea. They write the headlines, check the veracity of links, and ask tough questions before publication to protect my reputation after publication. They also ensure that my columns are published on schedule and monitor the comments.

While I am the subject expert, they are the publishing experts and make it their job to check my stance and, if needed, temper my tone. In working collaboratively, another advantage (beside receiving an education in publishing) is time freed up to explore new ideas.

When readers send particularly nice compliments, I always share them with the team who work hard behind the scenes.

Welcome the services of an editor

Whether you are just beginning or are a more practised writer, don't hesitate to use the services of an editor. As previously mentioned, a trusted colleague or friend may be sufficient to read short pieces (such as a column) to check they are interesting and accessible. But anything longer requires dedicated time (and fair remuneration) to obtain useful feedback.

When in the throes of self-doubt, I politely asked a writer friend for help and he obliged with tremendous warmth and excellent advice. Alas, my temporary high at his validation was soon replaced by my original doubts and the mix of good and bad feelings was discombobulating. This is very common, which is why objective scrutiny matters. After burning energy on my writing, my pressing question to an editor is often something I would not expect a loyal friend to answer truthfully: 'Is this really lame?'

Nothing replaces good writing, but a fine editor can take it up a few notches. I recommend putting in your best effort before seeking editorial comment. A few of my friends and writing students who don't publish regularly and want to improve their chances have used the services of a freelance editor to stay on track.

A note of caution. The job of a good editor is to improve, not replace your work. Whenever an editor's well-intentioned suggestions have diluted my voice, altered the tone or sometimes, the meaning of my writing, I have resisted with alacrity. A strong relationship with an editor entails freedom of input on both sides. The best outcome is when your work requires progressively light editorial touches.

TIPS

1. Before seeking an editor, put in your own best effort.
2. Soak up editorial advice and with time, you will need less of it.
3. A good editor will refine but never replace your voice.

What I Wish I Had Done for a Grieving Father

8 March 2025

New England Journal of Medicine

'Doctor, I mean no disrespect, but why am I even here?'

No patient wants to 'belong' to a geriatric oncology clinic, but over the years I've developed an acceptable explanation: 'As people get older, they develop a variety of problems. The aim of this clinic is to help older people with cancer take advantage of cancer treatments while shielding them from dangerous side effects.'

Noting the patient's name and slight accent, I offer to get an interpreter.

'Why?' he retorts. 'My English is perfect.'

Kicking myself, I hastily explain that half my patients require an interpreter and that I meant no insult.

The man, who is nearing 80 years of age, has gone for a routine vascular review and emerged with a finding of a liver mass. Noting that the mass appears to be malignant and unresectable, and the patient asymptomatic and disinterested, the surgeon sends him to me. The patient says he had no idea he was having a cancer workup – he just kept doing as he was told.

Patients attending this clinic answer questions regarding their coexisting conditions, functional fitness, emotional wellbeing, nutritional status and social support, since all these factors influence decisions about cancer care. The man's responses show him to be functionally fit and a candidate for treatment.

'They think it's some kind of cancer.'

'Yes, we would need a biopsy to find out more.'

'Not for me,' he says.

I remind myself that if I keep quiet instead of jumping in with 'but why?' I will soon find out.

But now we are sitting in total silence. He is staring at me, as I steal glances at him. I feel on edge but don't know why. I remind myself that an emergency button is situated at my knee.

'I would never have chemotherapy because I know how it destroys people.'

I make eye contact. And he starts sobbing.

'Wait, do I know you?' I ask.

'You remember how chemotherapy destroyed my daughter's life? After I see you, I am going to her grave.'

There is no imaginable way to say aloud what I'm thinking: *Of course! My team treated your daughter many years ago, but you were so much younger and more vital then. She was unforgettable; it's just that I never expected to see you here.*

'I am sorry,' I say, desperately hoping that this meagre expression will convey the pulsating intensity of my feeling.

His daughter was the apple of his eye, a middle-aged woman with a mild acquired brain injury and a placid disposition. Her 'good prognosis' cancer didn't behave as promised. As her metastases landed in inconvenient places, we kept chasing them with chemotherapy, radiation and increasing doses of opioids. But the gains we made always seemed to come at a high cost.

She could reliably report the symptoms she was experiencing – pain, lethargy, hunger and headaches. But when metastases pressed on her spinal cord and paralysed her legs, it fell to her father to appreciate the true extent of the threat to her life expectancy.

The relationship between oncologists and patients is serious and sacrosanct at one level and utterly simple and moving at another. I recall many of my patients with great fondness, for all sorts of reasons – the woman who brought a delectable home-baked cake to every visit even when she was nearing death, the man who shared travel recommendations when he could no longer fly, the patient who delivered birthday flowers in pouring rain, the one who brought baby clothes on my first day back from maternity leave. But my abiding memory of my experiences in the daughter's case is that as she became weaker and our treatment options diminished, her father began arriving clutching a piece of paper. The paper contained a number: his bank balance. He would surreptitiously press it into our hands so we knew to spare no expense in keeping his precious child alive.

His magical thinking broke my heart, in a country with universal healthcare, where public-hospital cancer treatment is free. Try as we might to reassure him, his foreign upbringing convinced him that with enough money, one could buy life.

Those conversations are echoing in my ears now.

'It's OK to not want treatment,' I say, 'but could I introduce you to palliative care?'

At the end of her life, his daughter was bed-bound and required home hospice for weeks that seemed like years. Cruelly, the number on the piece of paper had kept growing as her reserve faded.

'I don't want to go near palliative care,' he says fiercely.

I move to a final appeal.

'Then can I bring you back here to keep an eye on you?'

'No way,' he says. 'I will go without treatment and with peace.'

His expression of horror at my suggestions mixed with consideration for my feelings says it all: oncologists are no friends of his.

With a heavy heart, I see him out to visit his daughter's grave.

I hate to admit that my first reaction is one of surprise. I would say that his daughter received excellent care from a team that earnestly dwelled on her problems. I remember our visits being long and our sympathies abundant. And though I did not expect plaudits after she died, I feel a little pained that her father exclusively remembers the bad bits, now with ramifications for his own care. It feels like a delayed review that has downgraded me to an F where I'd given myself a B.

As the weeks go by and my calls to him go unanswered, I struggle to reconcile the world of professionals who believe they did their best with that of patients and caregivers who disagree. At such times, it's tempting to dismiss the latter as thankless or console ourselves that things might have gone far worse without our intervention.

But before I become indignant, I try to put myself in the father's place. His terminally ill daughter didn't fully comprehend her own situation, which left him in the invidious position of serving as both her physical caregiver and her psychological shield. Every piece of bad news had to travel through him to reach her. He had to decide how much to tell her and when, interpret her every wish and goal. The burden must have been oppressive.

So when we thought we were presenting sophisticated treatment options, he could only perceive us asking him to shoulder more decisions. Although I believe we were kind, our kindness was measured out in clinic time — not nearly enough to pierce his loneliness. And whereas money had helped him purchase his daughter the softest clothes and the gentlest music, it had proved no match for bad biology.

Why You Need an Editor

Communication experts say that naming and acknowledging an emotion is a simple and powerful way of connecting with people. Of course we knew he was having a hard time, but I don't recall saying so to him very often; doctors like to fix problems, and his daughter's case was brimming with them. I also remember being so unsettled by his expectations that it felt easier to focus on her cancer. Now I wonder whether we sufficiently acknowledged the unfairness of the situation and grieved with him. Did we say, 'I know this sucks,' instead of 'Here is what you could do next'?

If I could hit replay, I would give no less time to the daughter but devote more to her father. I would expand the ring of social workers, palliative care clinicians and others to embrace him as well as her, knowing that her terminal illness would be ever-present in his life. At the end of every visit, I would look at him and tell him he was doing a great job.

All these years later, I want to pull him back from the brink of his own suffering and ask, 'What could we have done better?' But he isn't coming back. So the best I can do is never again assume that my care, no matter how high by my standards, will be received as intended.

Entering the second half of my career, I wonder how to keep improving. I can't help thinking that this little dose of humility could go a long way toward making my future patients – and their families – feel more fully seen and heard.

About this column

There is something deeply satisfying about writing for a publication and working with the same editor for 20 years.

I wrote this essay after inviting Debbie Malina to speak to my writing class, where she told the students that while writers often looked for novelty in writing (and glumly realised that every idea had been taken), it wasn't the idea so much as the writer's unique perspective that mattered.

Debbie's words inspired me to think of an old encounter that I couldn't let go of. While essentially about the art of medicine, the story is unique, poignant and holds important practical lessons.

It felt risky to admit my indignation about the father's perception of his daughter's care lest I sounded tone-deaf, but I found this admission the most honest avenue to discussing a better way forward.

As always, Debbie's expert touches helped put the emphasis in the right places. Her questions helped me separate fact from emotion. A self-imposed word limit disciplined me to live by the title of this book: *Every Word Matters*.

Debbie's continuous exhortation to use authentic expressions made me completely comfortable using a phrase like 'I know this sucks' instead of replacing it with something passive and sterile but not 'lowbrow'. To her credit, she left it in.

This is an apt place to mention why I chose the *Journal* instead of my usual home at the *Guardian* to publish this account. I wanted to illustrate the power of professionals to shape the patient encounter and remind my colleagues of how people remember our conduct years later. In this case, the message was best delivered to the people charged with the responsibility.

Essays published in the *Journal*, mine included, are often used as teaching tools for a range of healthcare professionals, a satisfying bonus for those who want their writing to reach a broad audience.

18

The Work and the Joy of Writing

'A good writer possesses not only his own spirit
but also the spirit of his friends.'
Friedrich Nietzsche

Upon reading an early draft of this book, my superb editor observed that I had made the work of writing sound too easy. She commented that in my telling, anyone with a hint of an idea and a whiff of willpower could muster a column. But to leave aspiring writers with this impression was to do them a disservice.

Having poured over two years into writing a book about writing, my immediate reaction was to feel defensive before stopping to consider her comment.

I realised that the book contained no record of the years of planning, thinking (and doubting) that had preceded the writing or the excruciating task of convincing the publisher.

There was no mention of all the times I had begged out of events, offended friends and colleagues, and put other matters on hold in pursuit of a deadline.

No published column has a footnote about drafts scrubbed, ideas scorned, or sleepless nights spent in service of writing.

In my case, a passion for writing has involved passing on career opportunities which entailed stopping writing for a public platform or at least restricting its scope.

Of course, we all have many guises and hence, claims on our attention. My editor also taught students and frustrated writers – she did not want me to gloss over the discipline of writing but show how I silenced the competing demands of my life to get writing done.

I appreciated her observation that if writing were so easy that anyone could do it, then my book was unnecessary. And if I made writing sound appealing but unachievable, then it would deflate writers looking for a way in.

Incidentally, her remark reminded me of a similar conversation when I wrote *What It Takes to Be a Doctor*.

This book was driven by a desire to better equip students who aspired to be doctors and who were subsequently disappointed or surprised to discover that the daily work of medicine was less glamour and more grit. I wanted to strip away the misconceptions and help students, their parents and advisers make an informed decision to enter medicine.

The draft went through many hands, but it took a colleague I did not know well to spot a problem. She said that my book had made medical school sound like an easier undertaking than she remembered. 'Maybe it wasn't for you,' she said, 'but I found many subjects hard to understand and the workload exhausting.'

Now that she was a faculty member overseeing medical student welfare, she didn't want any prospective student to underestimate the volume or difficulty of study.

Her words brought back the memories I must have suppressed after becoming a doctor.

There were many days when I would lock myself in my room in a shared house and study from dawn to dusk. My neck and back hurt from bending over my books. The floor was covered in loose papers and notes. The rotations involved long-distance travel, moving in and out of very basic hospital quarters, and constant preparation for exams, whose results would determine internship offers. In my final year of medical school, I was so preoccupied and busy that I was subsisting on bread and cereal.

My editor's astute observation made me wonder if my propensity to downplay the difficulties of a task is a mental adaptation to keep moving in writing and in life. But I would hate to misrepresent the work of writing, so I want to take pains to emphasise that writing demands commitment, patience and hard work (but is also a lot of fun).

Always be thinking about your writing

This was the affectionate admonition of my late medical school professor and prolific writer who supported my writing career in its earliest days.

My *Guardian* column is published once every two weeks, typically mid-week. Publication day is the one day I permit myself complete freedom from thinking about writing. The others are spent planning, writing or editing a column and having periodic anxiety about never having another good idea.

A part of me is always fretting about how to fit writing around my commitments as a doctor and mother, two things that figure uppermost in my mind. The busier months in the hospital, such as winter or when I am attending daily rounds, stretch me thinner than usual.

Despite doing it for years, carving out time to write still feels hard won.

Writing something isn't enough; I want to write well and better than the last time. A prolific television show creator once enthused about the importance of letting the mind run fallow to spark the best work. I love the concept – and from my minuscule practice of it during my walks in nature, believe in it – but in this phase of my life, there is not a lot of time to be fallow.

Like most people, every day of my week has certain set responsibilities. Direct patient care tops the list but there is no prolonged switching off from patient care, even if you are not physically present. Besides phone calls, emails, mentorship, meetings and administrative work, there is the imperative to keep up with the unprecedented rate of medical advances. In this era of advancement, I wouldn't want to see an oncologist who can't recall when she last read a journal or attended a conference.

I am an avid reader who reads a little every day, sampling news, fiction and non-fiction. Apart from writing a regular journal for myself, I also write one for my children, a ritual I started with my first pregnancy.

I hold my relationships dear; daily contact with serious illness and mortality has drilled into me the sacred importance of relationships that cannot be delegated to another time. I am proud that my modest but tight circle of friends and family are actively and deeply invested in each other.

It is well known that healthcare professionals, including oncologists, who regularly confront ethical dilemmas and tragedies have a high rate of burnout. As an avid believer in the power of exercise as a self-help tool for mental health, I start my day at the gym.

At the other end of the day, I am fiercely protective of my sleep because good sleep helps with every consequential decision, not to mention personal wellbeing.

When I think about eliminating one or more of my commitments to free up writing time, I can't think of streamlining things even more than I already do. I guess I want to be a writer by embracing, not excluding, the messiness of real life.

In my job, I treat people who often don't have the privilege of choice or agency. Their passion, and even their primary occupation and closest relationships, must take a back seat when they are dealing with a serious illness. My patients long to have a fraction of the freedoms many of us take for granted. This is why I will never complain about writing. I love to write. I make a choice to write – and hence, make time to write.

Writing habits that work for me

It has been important for my evolution to free myself from expectations about what it means to be a 'real' writer.

One is shedding the idea of strictly protected or scheduled writing time.

I write whenever and wherever I can. I save a copy of my writing on the cloud which allows me quick access wherever I am. When a patient is running late or cancels, I might write as few as two or three lines, still a form of progress. Sometimes, I stay back after work and add a few more lines. Gradually, a column takes shape.

I have written on the sidelines of the soccer pitch, netball court, rowing sheds and cricket grounds, often from the passenger seat of my car (the steering wheel obstructs my laptop).

I strongly encourage my children's sporting endeavours but rarely watch them. I have missed nearly every penalty shot, half-century and rowing finish and experience occasional guilt, especially when I am 'found out' by other parents to be writing in the car. As my children grow older, I write at the gyms and malls they visit. I am all for fostering their independence while improving my word count. My children are so sanguine about this that I have to wonder about the guilt mothers foist upon themselves.

Writing requires solitude. Even thinking about writing needs headspace and I fight for this whenever possible.

But we all choose our priorities. For me, every opportunity to have dinner together is priceless and increasingly rare as my children grow up, so I generally won't write at the cost of dinner.

Every parent knows the unparalleled opportunity provided by time together in the car. I will move most things for this.

As my parents age, I strive to give them my time, albeit a bit more selfishly. They are more willing to work around my writing and as fond parents, quite happy to read quietly in the same room while I write. Having said this, when I turn to writing, I focus on writing. I shut the door to my room, turn off my phone, park other concerns, and write.

Decades of student life have made me a very good rule-follower. Given homework, I will do it well and turn it in on time. The mere thought of being late reminds me of the stress of being on call and feeling vaguely restless. The fear of missing out afflicts doctors, too: why wouldn't it?

The philosopher Seneca anticipated this two thousand years ago when he observed that to be everywhere is to be nowhere.

The Work and the Joy of Writing

I am extremely selective about accepting weeknight social invitations and have learnt that the fear of being considered impolite mostly lives in our minds. People often note the virtues of networking but I find them noisy and unfulfilling. I don't drink because I don't enjoy the taste of alcohol. I suspect that the avoidance of many ordinary nights and morning hangovers have somewhat contributed to better writing.

At large events, I arrive punctually and leave early. Done politely and with consideration this doesn't seem to bother people, at least judging by the repeat invitations. I am much more at home with small gatherings which foster good conversations that inevitably fuel good writing.

Consequently, there is much to recommend writing as a way of connecting with the world.

One obvious cost of writing is that I don't have time to watch the screen in an age of great content. Reviews and recommendations flowing in and out of my life leave me feeling wistful. I watched *The West Wing* a full ten years after it ended. I am inching my way through *Young Sheldon* with my son. I never finished watching Harry Potter.

On a lighter note, I am obliged to mention that my writing habit is generously supported by chocolate. I am convinced that writing is a famishing activity. Fine chocolate, preferably white (the unhealthy kind) always resides in my bedside drawer, within easy reach of where I write. (The lesser quality ones inhabit the pantry, for the kids.) It is a family joke that I always save the last few pieces for the kids to absolve me of the guilt of consuming an entire block of chocolate in service of writing.

The art of keeping going

I have mentioned intrinsic motivation as a pillar of my writing. But this type of motivation doesn't always deliver – there are many days when the writing process is dispiriting and just a slog. Behind every work that I publish, especially with my books, there are a lot of scribbles, flawed drafts and rejections. To help myself, and hopefully other writers, I have tried to understand what to do when intrinsic motivation stalls.

I recently came across a new term, identity motivation, when I heard a psychologist explain that if we keep working on intrinsic motivation, another construct called identity motivation can fill in the gaps.

Identity motivation is a social psychological theory that explains how people's identities influence their actions and goals. It's based on the idea that we use our identities to make sense of the world and conduct ourselves accordingly. This idea resonates with me.

For instance, I have written six full drafts of this book that I can recall, having rid my memory of the earliest ones.

When the thought of another redo feels tedious, I remember that I value being a writer and want to feel proud of the final product. This reminder of my values tides me through.

But if the writing felt incongruent with my values, the smallest difficulty could suggest redoubled effort as pointless and the work 'not meant for me'.

It seems to me that the commencement speeches about following one's heart and chasing one's passion are fit – for commencement speeches. The actual work is hard for the novice writer, chef, athlete and surgeon. There are many great writers with stupendously unsuccessful starts – we only know about the ones who did not lose courage. A central tenet of productivity is the art of keeping going.

Writing helps me

Writing is not only fulfilling, it also helps me make sense of my world. Processing experiences and reflecting on the lessons makes me a better doctor, but more importantly, many of the same lessons make me a better person. Writing opens me up to different perspectives, greater understanding and empathy, essential ingredients for a meaningful life.

Explaining the nuances of my craft to others to create awareness and empower them feels like an extension of service to society. But the best part about writing is human communion. Many writers say that they avoid reading reviews and comments. I read every one of them and pay special attention to the ones that are challenging or even uncharitable. I love the fact that people care enough about a topic to engage in dialogue with each other and with me. They inspire me to become a better writer.

Medicine is widely respected as a helping profession. But I had never thought of writing as a similar vocation. Now, I see how our words also have the capacity to reach strangers and offer practical guidance, advice and solace. This is not why I began writing but it has turned out to be the best part of writing.

I want to leave you with the most moving, meaningful and instructive letter I have ever received in my time of writing for the public.

Every Word Matters

Dear Ranjana,

I just wanted to send you a message to thank you for your column in the *Guardian*. I am a 31-year-old stage IV cancer patient (liver, lung secondaries, highly chemo responsive but my time's pretty limited). There's not a lot of writing on cancer that I respond to, or that I think really gives me a better perspective on the disease than I already have after fourteen months of living with a death sentence, but your writing always moves me and teaches me something different. I learn about medicine, and the system, and the act of living, and the reality of dying.

I also really appreciate you talking about things from the medical professionals' side of things. I have a wonderful oncologist whom I adore and a liver surgeon who is dedicated and focused on trying to do the impossible, and actually operate on my horrendously screwed up liver – but there's always a feeling as a patient that, at the end of the day, the affection and kindness your doctors show to you is just a thing that they put on to make you feel like they care. But you've taught me that doctors are as human as they seem – an obvious thing but one that's easy to forget between the scans and the constant navigation of your body as a complicated problem, rather than as a human being.

This letter landed in my inbox ten years ago and I read it a few times every year. I promptly responded to the writer who unfortunately died very shortly after writing me this kind note. It is impossible to not be struck by this final act of generosity.

On the days I feel tired or uninspired, these words uplift me and remind me to keep moving.

May this be your reminder, too, that writing can serve a purpose beyond the self.

Acknowledgements

Writing a book is a solitary act but no book is truly created in isolation. By the time it reaches the world, it carries the imprint of many generous minds.

I am grateful to the whole team at Simon & Schuster and singularly to Jarred Noulton for your attention to detail in bringing this book home. Luke Causby from Blue Cork was patient and generous in designing the book cover.

Special thanks to Alex Green, Debra Malina, Lawrence Quartana and Jeff Seglin whose thoughtful involvement shaped my early ideas.

Bernadette Foley, Claire Forster and Andrea McNamara put their steadying hands on my shoulders exactly when I needed it. You are a credit to your profession.

I work with a committed team at the *Guardian*, whose faith in me and respect for my vocation inspires me to keep working with them.

I am constantly indebted to my readers who hold me to a high standard.

To my patients – without your trust and openness, there would be no stories. This is a privilege I never take for granted and I thank you for keeping me grounded.

I feel incredibly lucky to be surrounded by loyal friends through every high and low of writing and life.

To mention just a few: Kwai, Anu, Geraldine, Hanita, Eliza,

Brian, Sarika, Mugdha, Warren, Vicki, Debbie, Dinesha, Kon, Khemka, Wendy, Robyn and Coleen – thank you for being present.

Our beautiful dog, Odie, deserves credit for being a loyal and patient foot soldier throughout the gestation of this book.

The staunch support and boundless love of my family are the foundation of my life.

My achievements reflect the investment of my parents and the support of my brother and his family.

Finally, to Rohan, Anjali and Sachin – my greatest achievement. Your capacity for love, consideration and practical support in both the significant and the everyday moments make me endlessly proud.

This book, even more than the others, has been a true team effort. Thank you.

About the Author

Dr Ranjana Srivastava is a practising Australian oncologist, award-winning author and Fulbright scholar. Educated in India, the UK, the United States and Australia, she is the recipient of the Monash University Distinguished Alumnus of the Year Award, the JFK Merit Award from the Harvard Kennedy School and the Medal of the Order of Australia for her contribution to doctor–patient communication. Ranjana's writing has been published worldwide, including in *Time* magazine and *The Week*, and in prominent medical journals such as the *New England Journal of Medicine*, the *Lancet* and the *Journal of the American Medical Association*. Her columns in the *Guardian* on the intersection of medicine and humanity have been twice nominated as a finalist for the Walkley Awards for Excellence in Journalism. In 2024, Beehive News named her the top international health columnist for context and completeness out of a field of 15,000 journalists across 55 categories. Her acclaimed non-fiction books include *Tell Me the Truth* (shortlisted, NSW Premier's Literary Awards), *Dying For a Chat* (winner, the Human Rights Literature Prize) and *What It Takes to Be a Doctor* (finalist, The Australian Career Book Award).

www.ingramcontent.com/pod-product-compliance
Lightning Source LLC
Chambersburg PA
CBHW011129070526
44583CB00023B/2960